A Culture of Excellence!

A Culture of Excellence!

THE ART, PRACTICE, AND DISCIPLINE

OF BREAKTHROUGH LEADERSHIP

Fardad Fateri & James E. York

ISBN-13: 978-0-69209537-9

Acknowledgements

Writing this book was not a project for us but a ten-year journey of passion. It didn't take us ten years to write this book but our book is the emerging property of a ten-year incubation in organizational learning, organizational culture, and leadership. There are hundreds of people who have contributed to the growth and development of our work and all these individuals are worthy of acknowledgement relative to capturing the core principles of our framework.

First and foremost, I want to acknowledge my co-author, Jim York, who did a yeoman's job in being the key ambassador of our work. Jim has been using many parts of this book in workshops, seminars, webinars, and conferences. He not only "gets it" but he lives every part of our framework.

I want to extend my heartfelt gratitude to my colleagues in our trusted inner circle who spent many hours reading our work and providing honest, substantive, and meaningful feedback so our content is delivered cohesively and thoughtfully.

I also want to recognize many of our colleagues at various locations across the United States, including my colleagues in my "CEO Mentorship Program," for their insights, observations, suggestions, and feedback. We certainly learned from everyone and did our best to integrate guidance to make the book useable, understandable, and powerful.

ONWARD and UPWARD!

Fardad Fateri

Contents

Foreword and Introduction
by Fardad Fateri

What is leadership? What does breakthrough leadership look like? What is organizational culture, and why is it important? Why does culture matter? Why is culture the most important pillar of the best organizations in the world? What are the values that separate great organizations from those that continually struggle? What empowers people to produce peak performers when many others can only produce mediocrity? What behaviors separate ordinary people from extraordinary superstars? What helps some organizations to survive and excel over time while many others fail?

These questions have remained at the core of my academic and professional careers for the past thirty-five years. I have always been a student of leadership and culture, and I have had the privilege to study and to work under several of the greatest scholars and organizational leaders in the United States. I learned a great deal from the very best.

I have always known that when leadership and culture are effectively leveraged, they can create sustained organizational greatness. My deepest interest was in developing people and allowing them to test their capacity to create the best versions of themselves. I knew that, within the appropriate culture, people with passion, bandwidth, and ambition would excel, and when people excel, an organization consistently achieves its objectives.

We've created an amazing environment at International Education Corporation (IEC)! Our culture has allowed us to grow dramatically—more than many similar organizations in the same economic sector—and to survive periods of turbulence and extreme difficulty. We're able to continuously reinvent ourselves to get better over time. While many of our competitors were shutting down, declaring bankruptcy, and dismantling, we continued to thrive.

IEC is perfectly imperfect. Though we face challenges, mistakes, and problems, we continue to learn, evolve, and improve every single day. We are a true learning organization committed to our core values, to our thesis, and to our customers.

It's not magic, and it's certainly not luck. Our success comes from our organizational culture. It's what separates failing or mediocre organizations from those that survive, persist, and sustain greatness regardless of economic conditions. Greatness is not about financial prowess—it's about survival, consistency, and persistence during economic and societal turbulence.

In the following chapters of this book, my colleague and I explore, identify, and explain what helped International Education Corporation develop a culture where people come together and create a platform for continuous quality and process improvement. I know our experiences, learning, and attributes will provide insight to readers both personally and professionally.

Before joining IEC in January 2008, I was the chief academic officer at one of the largest market-funded higher education corporations in North America. I had a prestigious and powerful position matched by few others in the country. I was generously compensated, and my company's reputation was one of the best in the nation. But I was unhappy. I felt I didn't have purpose. I wanted to lead a professional life that truly mattered. So in 2007, I decided to leave.

In my search for purpose, I came across a small career education company with only nine campuses. It was in such serious financial trouble that it struggled to meet payroll every two weeks. However, I didn't let the small size or the poor financial health of this organization stop me from assessing its overall potential. I decided to visit all the campuses and meet the staff and faculty who had committed their professional careers to this organization. After visiting the campuses and meeting the people, I fell in love with the organization because it had passion. It was small, but it had a heart bigger than most conglomerates. I saw tremendous potential and an extraordinary future. Therefore, I decided to leave my prestigious post to work at IEC and make it my new home.

My friends and colleagues seriously questioned my judgment for making such a poor career move. Some even wondered about my sanity! Who would leave a prestigious senior executive position at a multibillion-dollar corporation to join a small and almost bankrupt organization? But I made the life-changing decision to join IEC because I knew then what I know now: that IEC would allow me to have purpose and to create a culture where I and others like me could lead lives that truly matter.

Since January 2008, IEC has been through several dramatic architectural transformations; we had to reinvent ourselves multiple times to remain relevant and current. Although our name hasn't changed in the past ten years, we have evolved materially every year to survive. We went from a small organization struggling to meet payroll to one of the largest systems of private postsecondary career education in North America.

Neither I nor anyone else at IEC will ever claim that we are great or are the best; these are unacceptable words at IEC. We strive to become the best, though we know that's an unreachable destination for those who want to remain in business for decades. Over the years, remaining humble has made us vulnerable, and that vulnerability has allowed us to accept the brutal facts, learn continuously, enjoy the leadership of new top talent, and grow with quality and integrity—no stories, no excuses, no finger pointing, and no fluff.

Everything we've achieved at IEC was made possible only because of our culture, a culture we all built together. Our values and our identity allowed us to ascend through the good times and to survive during turbulent times. We are not smarter or better or more talented than anyone else, but at

IEC, we all share values that have empowered each of us to be the CEO of our position.

And here's the secret: anyone can build a culture that fuels success and breakthrough. I really mean that. It's why we wrote this book. In the coming chapters, you will learn the key values that can create and sustain greatness within any organization. We won't discuss any fancy theories or formulas but will instead focus on actual concepts that have helped IEC become an amazing organization and our people become breakthrough leaders. We will give you real-life examples of how our values have helped us get through very difficult times and leverage opportunities to achieve peak performance.

If you choose to adopt these lessons, values, and habits, you too can transform yourself personally and professionally to become the architect of your future. In almost every case, you have the choice to become accountable for the success of your department, your unit, your division, your region, your organization, and your own life. You can choose to be awesome!

Are you ready to embark on a path of personal and professional reinvention? Join us in this journey of discovery.

Onward and upward!

1

Culture Is a
State of Mind

Culture Is a State of Mind

Welcome! The first step of this journey is to define *culture*. Culture can mean a lot of different things to different people. To one person, it is how to hold the wine glass during a wine-tasting event. To another, it means knowing how to dress to "fit in" with one's peers.

Culture is as much a state of mind as it is anything else. It is how we think, act, and breathe. If we want to see personal or professional transformation, we have to create a culture of excellence—for ourselves, for our families, for our work teams, for our organization.

Many times, we think of culture as a *passive* concept, something that just *is*. It's something that we experience as a set of norms established by something or someone else. We operate within a particular culture without giving it much thought.

After all, the only important thing is that we follow the rules. Right?

Don't be fooled! We can create our own culture. Culture is a state of mind that we create, nurture, and preserve. We all have the opportunity to create the culture we live in by cultivating new norms for how we act, think, and behave.

If an organization can create its own culture of excellence, so can you!

Merriam-Webster's online dictionary defines *culture* as "the integrated pattern of human knowledge, belief, and behavior that depends on the capacity for learning and transmitting knowledge to succeeding generations" and "the set of shared attitudes, values, goals, and practices that characterize an organization."[1]

Without a doubt, organizational culture is one of the most important components and drivers of greatness. Top talent, viable strategy, and a thoughtful business thesis are great, but without a unified culture that colleagues believe in, organizations fail. On the flip side, organizations that have

---

1   *Merriam-Webster,* s.v. "culture," accessed April 10, 2018, https://www.merriam-webster.com/dictionary/culture.

a culture everyone understands often become the most reputable and successful organizations in their field! It is not about good or bad, right or wrong; it's all about sharing critical values that define the organization and encourage every single colleague to act and behave as one.

In organizations of excellence, leaders focus on cultural fit before any other consideration. When we interview leadership candidates for a position with IEC, the discussion revolves around their ability to thrive in our professional culture. Of course, the candidates must have the basic experience and expertise to do the job, but that's secondary to ensuring they'll be a good fit in the environment. Leaders understand it's essential for a candidate to support their organizational culture; if they don't, they will fail. Again, and we can't re-iterate enough: it's not about right or wrong, good or bad, it's about cultural fit.

For example, if a candidate has an autocratic, top-down, dictatorial leadership style, they most likely will not fit in a very inclusive, participatory, and communicative culture. The breakthrough organization and everyone in it is committed to their core values! Leaders must work tirelessly to make sure their values cascade down to all levels of the organization and are practiced consistently by every team member.

Now, let's take a peek at a little background so we can "set the stage" for our discussion.

How International Education Corporation Defined Its Culture

It's difficult to say exactly when we realized we had something special going on at IEC. At some point, though, we recognized there was something unique and powerful about our culture. Something was happening that we hadn't experienced in other organizations. The colleagues of IEC were all fully engaged in the success of our customers and our campuses. Was it passion? Was it spirit? Was it commitment? What was it, exactly? It seemed so elusive at the time! No one had taught us how to capture a culture, so we became culture pioneers.

We knew we had to find a way to "bottle" our culture to make sure we could share its uniqueness with all our employees, particularly new colleagues. We had to somehow capture and define the magic that was happening. That wasn't an easy task, I can assure you!

Our initial method was to bring our IEC leadership team together from across the company; we came together to define the uniqueness of the organization. We all got together in a comfortable and quiet location and examined the qualities that made us different from any organization any of us had ever worked with before.

The outcome was an extraordinary set of values, principles, and concepts that we captured in a statement called "We the People of IEC." This document is posted on the organization's internal website and still serves as a guide to each and every member of the organization, regardless of experience, title, or location. In short, every single member of the IEC team is exposed to our culture from day one!

Following is an excerpt from the document (see Appendix A for the full statement):

- We lead through recognition, gratitude, appreciation, praise, and inspiration.
- We have heart.
- We love to serve.
- We manage and lead by example.
- We regularly measure and monitor all we do in order to achieve top performance.
- We make thoughtful but quick decisions, and we take action.
- We are flexible, agile, and nimble, and we exhibit structure and discipline in all we do.

- We are passionate about student success.
- We embrace teamwork and strongly encourage open communication.
- We integrate regulatory compliance in all we do and never treat it as an event.
- We care deeply about the success of our students and our colleagues.
- We have a strong commitment to excellence and will never settle for less.
- We have an appetite for growth with quality and integrity.
- We are always hungry for more.
- We will never be perfect and know we can always improve.
- We learn and grow from our mistakes.
- We always embrace greatness.
- We make grassroots investments that lead to student and employee success.
- We have a sense of urgency.
- We take personal accountability and look within for solutions.
- We attract, hire, and develop the best talent.
- We seek support and assistance when needed.
- We promote from within.

- We empower "all" of our people to take ownership and serve.
- We praise in public and coach in private.
- We are close to our business and we know the numbers.
- We have enterprise-wide transparency.
- We face and accept the brutal facts and take action to address them effectively.
- We follow up and follow through on our commitments, priorities, and responsibilities.
- Our team at the corporate office is aligned to serve and to support the campuses.
- We are mindful of the big picture, which keeps us focused at all times.
- We exhibit determination in all we do; we never give up.
- We demonstrate strong communication at all times with no silos.
- We focus on all levels of the educational model to provide a top-quality student experience.
- We have fun as a team and enjoy what we do.
- We focus on fundamentals.

- We are deliberate in our actions and are always focused on results.
- We are high-energy.
- We have a positive attitude.
- We have caring, supportive, and nurturing environments.
- We are super competitive.
- We always focus on our competencies, keeping students at the heart of our enterprise.
- We take deliberate steps to celebrate achievements regularly.
- We operate under "One Standard of Excellence" in all we do within all departments.
- We take pride in our work.
- We are 24/7.
- We are "grown-ups."
- We are respectful.
- We are professional.

How to Cultivate Your Culture
(Should We Say, "Culture-Vate"?)

Because culture is a state of mind, it is accessible to anyone. Our experience in driving an enterprise-wide culture can be applied to both individual and organizational success. By paying attention to certain concepts and principles, such as humility, ownership, accountability, and more, you too can create a successful environment. You can impact your own future. You can even influence an entire organization!

We promise that if you implement the values, concepts, and principles we present in this book, you will not only enjoy a renewed sense of hope for your future, you will actively create your future! You will create a culture of excellence. There are some foundational things you need to commit to when you embark on designing and implementing culture in your own organization.

Get Everyone on Board

At the organizational level, it's essential that you get buy-in from everyone. In a multisite- and multistate-distributed organizational structure such as ours (or indeed in many other organizations in today's changing marketplace) it is absolutely vital that each and every one of our colleagues is on board with the direction of the organization. How do you achieve that? Certainly by having robust processes and procedures. But the most essential component we've realized is you need to have team members be a part of—*rather than apart from*—all the decisions made and actions taken.

Plan for a Revolution!

We would also be a bit remiss if we didn't warn you: plan for a revolution! Once your team members and employees adopt these concepts, they can't help but act as change agents for them! You will see. They are really very simple, and they make sense. If we can do it, so can you!

Expect and Celebrate Redundancy

As you read through the material, you'll notice that certain themes seem to appear more than once. You might think to yourself, *Didn't we just discuss this?* You're absolutely correct! A culture of excellence requires attention to detail, certainly, but it also requires redundancy. Frequent repetition of core practices and concepts is vital in order to energize your role, your team, your organization, your company, and your enterprise! So when you say to yourself, "Hmm . . . I've seen that before," you're probably right! Just remember, it is by design, not by accident.

Ask yourself what values, practices, beliefs, and behaviors should be repeated in your own team, department, and organization. How can you use redundancy to your advantage as you cultivate a culture of excellence?

Strive to Become an Organization of Excellence

At IEC, we are an organization of excellence.

Organizations of excellence care deeply about their culture and take many deliberate steps to ensure all core values are alive and well. Our experience has been that culture is by far the number one predictor of organizational success.

As you read through these concepts, take the time to digest them and self-reflect. For many of us, our natural tendency is to read or listen to guidance and then agree that the people around us are not behaving as expected. But leadership excellence does not allow for us to be a critic or spectator! In what ways can you more fully embody the values of your organizational culture? First, hold yourself personally accountable to produce necessary changes in your approach! Then you'll be in a position to hold your organizational leaders to the same rigorous standards.

We know that an organization is a living, dynamic, collective entity made up of the values and colleagues within that organization. We might even think of organization as an extension of an organism in that it is "alive" and vital. It requires a nurturing and healthy environment in which to thrive!

Excellence Is the Driving Force of Successful Organizational Culture

We've been using the word *excellence* a lot in only a short time. That's because excellence is the driving force of successful organizational culture. Raise the standards of your values to the highest level and enforce those standards consistently across all levels of the organization. This is what it means to hold values of excellence. And a culture of excellence is what drives success.

You might have heard of the adage, "The true measure of a person's character is what they do when no one is looking." We know that effective leaders perform with integrity, whether others see it or not! So then we might adjust the adage to say, "The true measure of a good leader is what they do when no one is looking!"

What about you? Do you consistently embody your organization's values with integrity? Do you strive to be an effective leader? Think of specific examples, of a time no one was watching but you did the right thing. Think of a time you failed to achieve your highest standards and what you learned from that experience. It is important to be honest with yourself on both accounts. Successful leaders are brutally honest with themselves! This is how, day after day, they hold themselves and their teammates to the highest standards.

A Culture of Excellence Demands Leaders of Excellence

A culture of excellence requires—in fact, demands—leaders of excellence. You can't achieve the one without the other. Jim Collins refers to such leaders as "breakthrough leaders" (Collins & Porras, 1994). For the purposes of our discussion, the term "breakthrough leaders" is synonymous with our own term, "leaders of excellence."

An organization's leaders of excellence fuel these cultural values over time. But being a leader of excellence is more than just having high standards. How exactly does a person become a respectable leader able to guide others and direct the course of organizational culture over time and distance?

2

Leaders of
Excellence

Be the CEO of Your Position!

We like to say that being a leader of excellence means becoming the "CEO of your position." Being the CEO of your position is something anyone can do. In fact, it's essential in order for their organization to thrive.

It sounds pretty lofty, doesn't it? But what does it mean to be the CEO of your position? After all, how many of us have ever considered ourselves a CEO?

The key to embodying this mindset is *ownership*. Own it! Create your own destiny! Take charge! Be accountable! At the end of the day, you are the one accountable to yourself, your team, your family. *You* are the one in charge.

Being the CEO of your position means you authentically own your responsibilities, you refuse to accept mediocrity, and you take swift but thoughtful action at all times to influence favorable change and to meet and exceed expectations.

When you are the CEO of your position, you are a breakthrough leader! Breakthrough leaders don't do things to please others. Breakthrough leaders want to produce peak performance in all areas to meet the high standards they hold for themselves (Collins & Porras, 1994).

Leaders of excellence are tougher on themselves than on anyone else. They rate themselves every day and every week by asking themselves honest questions. Most importantly, they always face the brutal facts and take deliberate action to achieve organizational expectations. Breakthrough leaders don't wait for greatness to knock on their doors, they create greatness! So don't wait. Be powerful, be bold, and be audacious. Create your own destiny!

Organizations often tell their leaders in the field that they are in charge, but they don't actually let those leaders make any real decisions! Why does that happen? The organization doesn't fully trust its leaders, or it feels it will have greater control by micromanaging. The consequence is that it does not give field leaders the chance to be excellent. To be clear, excellence does not mean perfection.

An organization of excellence expects its leaders to make mistakes or to fail from time to time. That is how we learn and grow as an organization. On the other hand, an organization of excellence does not allow mistakes and failures to persist over time without seeking solutions or improved results.

Leaders of excellence thrive on autonomy, opportunity, and the chance to prove they can be the CEO of their position. These proven leaders don't allow results to suffer. As they overcome failure and learn from mistakes, the organization learns and grows too.

So leverage these concepts of autonomy, opportunity, and excellence to produce peak performance. Be assertive, aggressive, in charge, and in control. Don't focus on excuses about why you can't be the best. Focus on solutions that will make you the best! Regardless of your job title, be the CEO of your position and you'll thrive.

Leaders of Excellence
Take Ownership

Leaders of excellence treat their colleagues and teams as owners of their business and expect their behavior to reflect true ownership. Ownership is not about power and control but about caring for your business, your team members, and your results. Ownership means being very hands-on with everything that happens in your business. Leaders do whatever it takes to achieve expected results with quality and integrity; no stories, no excuses, and no fluff.

A breakthrough leader isn't passive; he or she strives to optimize processes and achieve the best outcomes. A breakthrough leader maintains a sense of urgency to move agendas forward and maximize productivity with tasks, projects, initiatives, and assignments. He or she is organized, structured, timely, and disciplined and always expects the same of others.

By maintaining extreme focus on your mission, goals, and priorities, you ensure the best chance of reaching your goals. Then set expectations for your team members, who will follow your lead. A central responsibility of leaders of excellence is managing their teams. This requires a robust and compassionate approach. What are some essential aspects of managing your teams well?

Communicate Expectations and Needs of the Team

As leaders of excellence, we understand expectations. Expectations help us define the direction our colleagues must take. We make these expectations very clear so that colleagues can fully understand what our common goals are, what is important, and what is not. We over-communicate outcomes, results, and expectations to our colleagues at all times. We expect that others do the same with their team members at their sites, offices, regions, divisions, and organizations.

We expect top performers to help their peers achieve the same, and we expect those struggling with results to reach out to peers at other sites, offices, and regions to solicit help. Pride and ego must not prevent us from raising our hands and asking our colleagues to help. Our top priority is to focus on our customers; we truly admire colleagues who have the courage to ask for help because that's a selfless act.

We always look at quantitative results to gauge effective management and leadership. Our saying, "fewer words and more numbers," can describe effective leadership. Results are the emerging outcomes of hundreds of decisions and actions. Results speak volumes about our work ethic, focus, ability, experience, vigor, commitment to excellence, accountability, pride, passion, sense of urgency, and leadership.

Celebrate the Team's Successes

We love what we do! Our focus is always on making sure we have the best learning communities, we have the best staff and colleagues, and that we serve our customers at the highest level. We expect the same from others.

Organizations of excellence thrive through hard work, passion, vigor, focus, ownership, ambition, personal accountability, and leadership! Top quantitative results are outcomes of a superior culture, one that is anchored in personal accountability, a sense of urgency, true ownership, hard work, competitiveness, passion, regulatory compliance, teamwork, a strong appetite for winning, integrity, and an environment that cares deeply about customer and colleague success. We all must always achieve top results!

And when your organization achieves top results, NEVER forget to celebrate them! Much good can come from simply letting others know when they are successful. Announce the victory! Use the team's achievement to develop momentum and continue their current trajectory of success! After all, what can be more motivating than truly succeeding . . . than truly making a difference?

Confront Team Members
When They Fall Short

As leaders of excellence, of course we want to inspire and motivate our colleagues publicly through repeated words of recognition and praise. However, should there be issues with performance and behavior, we coach our colleagues in private. Remember to praise in public and to coach in private.

As leaders of excellence, we know that no one is exempt from living the values and behaviors of a culture of excellence. If *we* think our boss or another executive is not following or living our values, might it be possible that our own direct reports are saying the very same thing about *us*? Ironically, in many cases it is those very same managers who complain about their supervisors, often getting the same complaints from their own direct reports! Let us all be real and act accordingly.

One of the more difficult roles you will have as a leader of excellence is to "confront the brutal facts." This sometimes requires difficult but respectful one-on-one communication with colleagues. While this can be a difficult process, it is also a very important component of effective leadership. Colleagues need to know where they stand.

That being said, colleagues also deserve to know what changes have to be made in order for them to be successful in the organization. After all, why wouldn't we want each and every colleague in our organization to be successful . . . ? Of course we do! But it requires effort and attention. This is something leaders of excellence do not shy away from. Leaders of excellence confront the brutal facts.

If you are reading this material, you are on the way to becoming a leader of excellence! To becoming the CEO of your position!

Leaders of excellence don't require additional or unnecessary attention from others in the organization. They know they need to produce at the highest level, and they monitor their own performance and the outcomes of their team. Strong leaders develop and empower strong teams through consistent and compassionate communication, celebration, and confrontation.

Being a leader of excellence means you authentically own your responsibilities, refuse to accept mediocrity, and take swift but thoughtful action at all times to influence favorable change beyond expectations. Leaders of excellence don't do things to please others; they want to produce peak performance in all areas to please themselves because their standards are much higher than others'.

Above all, leaders of excellence look to the organization's culture to guide them. Leaders rely on the organization's core values to inform others of their goals, priorities, processes, and behaviors.

3

Values of Leadership Excellence

What Are the Values of Leadership Excellence?

Each of us is capable of being a leader of excellence. But in order to be the CEO of your position, you must embody values that set you apart from your teammates. What are the values that make a leader of excellence?

Becoming a true leader of excellence starts with identifying who you are, what you stand for, and what you are about. It is about focusing on your DNA, your internal code, your values system of success. In the following pages, we'll share our IEC values system with you. As you explore what makes us leaders of excellence, ask yourself what attributes resonate with you? Which ones don't? What's missing from our list that you feel is at the top of your list of essential values?

Creating Urgency

Having a sense of urgency is a critical part of becoming a leader of excellence. You must have a clear timeline for your projects and you must feel a sense of internal pressure to complete tasks on time. Not only that, you feel the responsibility to create accurate, thoughtful, consistent, high-quality work. You don't just aim to meet deadlines—you strive to beat them! You make a habit of exceeding customer and organizational expectations. Leaders of excellence make sure they remain focused on work until the job is done right.

What separates average performers from great performers? The answer is always the same: hard work! Talent, skills, abilities, and aptitude are critical, but they aren't unique. It's hard work that delineates average performers from top performers. Nothing can ever replace hard work. You've heard the saying, "The harder I work, the luckier I get." It's true! Hard work, productivity, and performance are positively and strongly correlated, which means the harder you work, the more you will accomplish and the more successful you will be in achieving desired results. Hard work doesn't necessarily mean how many hours you spend in the office or what time you clock in or clock out; it's about what you do and the results you achieve while you are working!

Utilizing Intuition

Leaders of excellence carry a "no limits" mentality. They don't see any ceilings above them. They operate in a wide-open, spacious, and highly charged atmosphere. Ask these leaders for one, and they'll give you ten!

Don't allow anyone or anything to limit your thinking! Not only is this about numbers; it's also about taking initiative. Intuitive leaders see a need and work to find solutions. They don't let problems linger, they don't do only the minimum requirements, and they don't wait for someone else to notice a need. If they see room for improvement, they work to make it happen.

Think of the last time you asked someone to do something for you. Let's go with raking leaves, for example. You put in extra hours at work, you were exhausted, and you just needed some downtime. But it was late when you pulled into the driveway after work on Friday evening, and you saw the yard was a mess. Leaves were everywhere. Your community is under a "no-burn" ordinance, so you can't burn the leaves. The neighbors' yards looked green and perfect. The wind was blowing your leaves into their yards. The special Saturday trash pickup was the very next afternoon. The work had to get done, but you were out of energy. You were done. You were over it.

You asked your teenage son to rake the leaves as a special favor to you. He said he would after he got a few things from the store. Oh, boy. You had heard this before! You just knew nothing would get done.

Exhausted, you fell asleep for several hours, only to wake up, look out the window, and find that the yard was spotless! Not one leaf remained. There were no lawn bags left anywhere. Your front yard looked like a perfectly manicured golf course!

Upon investigation, you find out that your son's trip to the store was to get special lawn bags to get the yard done. Not only did he rake and bag the leaves, he took them to the local dump to dispose of them so you wouldn't have to worry about it. And he got the lawn mower and trimmers out to make sure the lawn looked just right.

He was acting as a leader of excellence! He was being intuitive and observant. He knew what had to be done and he accomplished his assignment and more! He went above and beyond. Just raking the leaves would have been a mediocre performance. Bagging, dumping, mowing, and trimming made it an excellent performance! No one asked him to go above and beyond. He just did it.

That's what leaders of excellence do. They don't brag about their initiative; they don't run around reporting what a great job they did. They get the work done, and then they move on to the next challenge.

The next time you are asked to perform a function, whether it be at work or at home, give your boss more than they asked for! Be a leader of excellence! Perform without limits.

Expressing Curiosity

Leaders of excellence are always curious. They wonder if their processes are effective. Is their work-flow at peak efficiency? How might they improve their management approach to raise team morale? This quality also gives rise to tenacity. Just because something has "always been done this way," it does not mean it has always been done the *right* way. When a strong leader sees an opportunity for improvement, they take the risk. Sometimes this requires speaking up when things do not seem right.

Do not accept a result if it seems wrong. Be willing to take the risk to raise the bar of achievement.

Being curious means asking a lot of questions! However, this doesn't mean that it's okay to be rude, disrespectful, or unprofessional. This is unacceptable behavior from a leader. Leaders set the tone for their team, department, and organization. As long as you act professionally and respectfully, you should never fear sacrificing what is right for your team or your business for fear of hurting feelings, making someone upset, and/or crossing chains of command. What you should fear is failure and defeat. So ask the questions that *matter*. This allows your colleagues to know that you care.

If you want results in a certain area, that's where you should direct your focus and curiosity. Interest from a leader signals team members to follow suit.

Instilling Accountability

Lead, follow, or get out of my way! Pretty strong words, right? Certainly passionate, to say the least!

Indeed, the importance of passion in leaders of excellence cannot be disregarded! Leaders of excellence are humble, communicative, consistent, respectful, and are team players . . . and they never wait to be told what to do! In a culture of excellence, superstars abound! They know what has to be done, and they go about doing it! They own it! They are accountable, so they get on with it! They ask for help when needed, but they are very clear that, when all is said and done, they are responsible for their own success and the success of their colleagues.

No exceptions! None! Zero!

A culture of excellence demands it!

Many who consider themselves accountable for outcomes and objectives often point the finger at other people's shortcomings when they fail. Truly accountable leaders accept the responsibility for getting the job done. No stories, no excuses, and no fluff. When leaders are accountable, they authentically feel like true owners of their positions, departments, stores, locations, regions, or sites. Leaders of excellence teach accountability by modeling it through ownership. If you don't point the finger, blame, tell stories, or make excuses, your team members won't either. You reinforce in your words and your actions the kinds of behaviors that are and aren't appropriate.

It is fine to make mistakes, but own mistakes and learn from them. Never criticize your colleagues for being weak or incapable; that's not the way to solve the problem. Leaders of excellence look within and master their responsibilities first before disciplining others.

Being personally accountable is a huge factor in separating leaders and organizations. An attitude of accountability demands action. It demands the leader be hands-on and engaged. There's a fine balance, but leaders of excellence know how to delegate. They trust their team, they don't micromanage, and they share responsibility to get things done. You are in charge and you know how to do the work. You are not a broker. You are not a consultant. When you are truly the CEO of your position, others around you will understand what the role really means and will learn from your behavior.

Leaders of excellence lead primarily by example. They don't feel the need to brag about being accountable and they don't micromanage! Their behavior, actions, and qualities speak for themselves. You may hear people expressing how "accountable" they are, but later they're the ones complaining to coworkers or blaming others for their failures. Have you ever had that experience?

Complaining to peers may be therapeutic and perhaps even reassuring, but it produces negativity, discomfort, and low confidence. So if you feel down on some days, go in front of a mirror and say, "It is all the boss's fault because they just don't get it, and . . . plus . . . I am awesome!" Then, once you are done, get on with it! Leaders who are powerful, assertive, and strong make decisions, take action, and execute plans. Everything else is just fluff.

Leaders of excellence take action and do not wait or hope and pray for something or someone to save the day. When dealing with issues, problems, and opportunities that manifest themselves in the form of inferior quantitative results, it is more important to take action and make a mistake than to be a passive leader. When your teammates observe a leader's inaction and see him or her hoping and praying for miraculous improvements without some kind of intervention, they lose confidence.

When you observe results below expected

levels, that's your cue to take action. It is okay to make a mistake, but inaction will lead to failure and defeat. You might have observed that some team members are more afraid of making a mistake than they are afraid of actually failing. Unfortunately, due to their fear of making a mistake, they fail by way of inaction! When faced with these two options, always take the former. Take action!

In an organization of excellence, being accountable for making a mistake earns the respect of colleagues. Ownership is an important pillar of a culture of excellence. Owning the mistake provides a level of humility and vulnerability, both of which require strength of character. Leaders of excellence have strength of character.

A great example of this concept of accountability played out in our organization. One member of the IEC team had heard the phrase, "No stories, no excuses, no fluff" several times. She was certain that she knew exactly what it meant until she stumbled and failed on a project. She was used to being a superstar, a winner, and now suddenly she didn't feel as if she was winning! Ouch! She spent time justifying it to herself with excuses like, "I did not get stupid overnight, so it cannot be my fault." She spent more time further explaining to herself why she failed, who was to blame, and so on, rather than focusing on what resources and partnerships she needed in order to be successful. She was more interested in sharing all of the "he said she said" stories than focusing on a plan to achieve the outcomes.

Her supervisor asked her, "What does it matter who is right and who is wrong if you are not winning? The world is not fair! Life is not fair! Business is not fair! Sometimes we have to make decisions that are in the best interest of the customer and the organization and not what is in the best interest of one given person. Do you want to be right, or do you want to win?"

The colleague soon discovered it was time to start winning rather than focusing on being "right." She realized if she wanted to win, she must not worry about the problems so much as she should solutions so as to leverage resources and partnerships to achieve the best outcome. That is accountability.

Using Perspective

It is likely you work in a "team" industry. It doesn't matter how an *individual* performs if the *team* fails. For example, you may have one fantastic sales professional who consistently does very well, but if all others on the team do not contribute proportionately then the team will fail. On a different level, a department may do very well, but if other departments do not then the bigger team will fail. A leader of excellence has a sense of perspective. They care not only about their own success but also about the success of their division, region, and company as a whole, and they strive to optimize performance beyond themselves to ensure the success of the organization.

For example, a sales team may perform well, but if your product or service is not packaged in a timely manner, if your customers don't have a positive experience and decide to do business with another company, then the larger team will fail. A leader of excellence will focus on areas and outcomes that display the company's success! Leaders of excellence are thoughtful about not functioning within silos; they seek to work collaboratively across all boundaries. Everyone—every single colleague—must work together to ensure the organization functions as ONE. Leaders need to own the success of their colleagues within every department, every site, every location, and every region. Please remember, to all outsiders, the company must appear as ONE. Leaders of excellence act and behave as one!

Working Hard

Work ethic, pride, and care are subjective values; they are relative and based on personal experience. Leaders of excellence have an unwavering commitment to a common standard, a common set of processes of excellence across the enterprise. At IEC, we refer to this as "One Standard of Excellence"— one standard—to aspire to, a common standard across the organization measured by quantitative benchmarks. Those who meet and exceed expectations and work hard have pride in what they do. They simply care more than others. All fantastic ideas, processes, tools, and resources can only be meaningful when grouped with hard work, pride, and care.

People may tell you they work hard, they have pride, and they care a great deal. That may very well be the case! But these attributes can only be shown through meeting an organization's quantitative expectations. So if you, your teams, or your departments are not meeting expectations and standards of excellence then you must work harder, you must show more pride, and you must care more.

Working in your field of choice can be extremely rewarding! It may be that your role is your passion; perhaps it is your calling. Maybe you hold a unique and unusual position that requires a great deal more effort, passion, care, sacrifice, commitment, and sweat equity than those of your peers. Whatever the case, be the CEO of your position. Own it. Do your work with excellence!

Let's look at an example to illustrate the difference between caring and caring more.

You are the customer representative in a large building supplies store. This store caters to both women and men who love to come in and dream of home improvement. Every aisle has a surprise! Every aisle contains something they could use. A person could spend an afternoon here. It is one of a national chain of such stores and it is well known for quality and for having a HUGE inventory.

As the customer representative, your job is to walk the store and see if you can help customers with their needs. After all, if they are looking for a specific size of nuts and bolts, for example, it could literally take the customer half an hour just to find the right section!

Customer Evelyn has two children with her. One of them is in a baby carrier; the other is a two-year-old. Evelyn looks harried and confused, so you quickly approach her and ask how you can help.

Good for you! You think to yourself, *what great service I provide!*

Evelyn asks you where she can find a specific set of nuts and bolts. Her husband is in the middle of a big project at home and has asked her to hurry over to the store and pick these up for him so the project can continue. He is short on time, so this is very important for the timely finish of the project.

Proving what a great customer rep you are, you point Evelyn to Aisle 14, where all of the nuts and bolts are! You even brag about the thousands and thousands of sizes and shapes of nuts and bolts you have in inventory. Surely she will find what she needs. You feel good about helping her as she walks toward Aisle 14 with one kid in hand and one kid in tow. You're proud of yourself—you did your job. You showed how much you care!

But . . . were you a leader of excellence? Did you act as the CEO of your position? Well, don't feel too good just yet! A leader of excellence goes above and beyond.

To care is good. To care more is excellent.

To care is to tell Evelyn which aisle the nuts and bolts are in and point her and the young kids in the right direction. To care is to be courteous, respectful, and informative. However, a leader of excellence cares more. To care more is to walk with Evelyn over to the exact section in Aisle 14 and to stay and answer any questions she may have. To care more is to help her pick out the nuts and bolts she needs or to call for an expert in the department to assist if you do not have the required knowledge to do so. You are available in case she needs to call her husband and ask questions about exactly what is needed. You can see this is really important to them!

Leaders of excellence care *more*. We create an atmosphere where the customer doesn't feel like they are bothering us. To care more is to make them comfortable enough to allow you to assist them.

See the difference?

Leaders of excellence care more because their organization of excellence cares more.

Operating with Humility

Often, when we think of humility, we imagine someone understated, quiet, and reserved—maybe even weak. But that is not our definition of humility. And that is certainly not the role of humility in a culture of excellence!

Humble leaders are successful leaders because they make themselves vulnerable to honest and continuous self-assessment and feedback from others. They never become victims of ego given to delusions of grandeur. Authentically humble leaders are never satisfied with being awesome yesterday or today! They are obsessed with continuous learning to ensure excellence at all times.

Leaders of excellence are never satisfied with just being good or with just meeting expectations; they always want to WIN in everything they do. They understand that self-improvement is the path to exceeding expectations. Leaders of excellence think like this: *Well, I agree that we are good, but we need to do a lot more to be great.* That's humility in action! Certainly, leaders of excellence are high achievers and don't confuse being good with being great.

Humility is a learned trait of courageous

leaders. Humility is learned when character is tested against difficult struggles. Humility allows us to learn, to sympathize, to empathize, to grow, to influence, to make mistakes, to admit to our faults, to collaborate, to be inclusive, and to earn the respect of our colleagues. This trait will let others inside and outside of the organization know that the leadership of the organization is approachable and human. Superstars want to follow leaders they respect and look up to.

When you think about it, accepting the gift of humility will free you from the curse of excessive ego! When your state of mind is one of humility then focusing on creating solutions and serving your customers take center stage. That's where every leader should strive to be. Focus on solutions and not problems. Being humble will allow you to be in the proper state of mind to learn, solve difficult problems, and chase excellence.

To position yourself effectively as a leader of excellence, you must have the courage, confidence, and mental strength to be humble. With humility, you will have the opportunity to be thoughtful, respectful, and inclusive. Your management style will leave room for the input of others and you will lead with compassion. Always remember that sarcasm, disrespect, rudeness, and authoritarian behavior in your management style are properties of arrogance and insecurity. These are all learned behaviors. Leaders of excellence must be humble but confident, treating customers and colleagues in alignment with the values of high-performing cultures.

Leaders of excellence create and enjoy an office and campus climate anchored in discipline, structure, achievement, and fun! Enjoy your high-performing culture! Embrace high expectations! Have fun!

Utilizing Wisdom

You have likely encountered a situation where you knew you were right and the other person was wrong, and you felt compelled to "make it right." You needed to let them know you were in the right and they were in the wrong. Wouldn't it be great to satisfy your ego? To go tell them where they were wrong? To put them in their place? Yes, indeed that would feel good! But is that the best thing?

Let's look at an example. Imagine you are a regional manager for an auto parts company across three states. You have an excellent sales director, Sandra, in one of your stores. Sandra is always at the top of the list. She is your number one! She is driven, successful, and a great leader of her sales team. Her processes are compliant. She has outstanding integrity. She loves her team and she loves the organization. Customers love her. Sandra does everything right. What a fantastic situation for both Sandra and the company!

At Sandra's recommendation, her daughter (Gina) applies to an entry-level administrative job at another location (the organization does not allow family members to report to each other). After all, like mother, like daughter, right? Wrong! The other location really doesn't care for Gina. The interview doesn't go well. Gina is discouraged, upset, and doesn't understand why she wasn't successful in the interview. After all, her parent is successful! Why isn't Gina?

Gina confides in Sandra. Or, more importantly, child confides in parent. Sandra, the parent, gets upset and threatens to quit the company if Gina isn't hired. As the regional manager, you might be offended. You may think, *Are you kidding me? Really? Who do you think you are?* You might take it personally and think to yourself, *Go ahead then! Quit! Who are you to tell me what to do?*

You feel quite self-righteous! After all that you have done for Sandra, how could she do this to you?

However, let's slow down and think about this for a minute. Would you rather be right, or would you rather have the best outcome? Let's decide by exploring the possible scenarios.

Scenario #1: We tell Sandra to go ahead and quit. Consider the consequences of that action:

- You lose your number-one sales director.
- Sandra is angry, resentful, and feels very

justified. She goes to your competitor and starts taking customers away from you.

- You have to find a replacement for Sandra. You'll have to take the time to train the new employee. In the meantime, you risk losing customers.
- Sandra's team is demoralized and becomes distracted.
- Sandra's team worries that her replacement won't be as supportive as Sandra.
- Sandra's team worries that something bad will happen to them too.
- You take the chance of Sandra calling members of your team to come over to her new company.
- The other location has to keep looking to fill the minor administrative position at the other location.

Scenario #2: Hire Gina for the entry-level administrative position at the other location. What are the possible consequences?

- You take the chance of frustrating the hiring manager of the other location.
- Sandra is happy, and her daughter is

happy. After all, it is an entry-level administrative position.

Of course, this is an imperfect scenario. You'll need to forgive its simplicity. But the concept holds true.

Leaders of excellence check their ego at the door. They always search for and work to achieve the best outcome!

As you read through the material, be sure to run this very important concept through your mind from time to time. Use it at home, use it at school, use it at work—even use it on your vacation! Don't we all love to be right? But if being "right" costs you in the long run, you need to weigh the damage to your ego against what best suits your family, your team, or your future!

As the CEO of your position, you must always seek the best outcome. The results will speak for themselves. You don't always have to prove that you're right!

Giving Respect

Another very important trait of a leader of excellence is respect.

Respect is the foundation of customer service. You cannot serve genuinely and fully when you don't respect your customers.

Leaders of excellence respect their colleagues, customers, and vendors alike, and hold them in the highest regard. There are no exceptions to this rule. Titles do not give anyone the right to be sarcastic, rude, degrading, and disrespectful in their communication or behavior. Titles do not define leaders of excellence; rather, behaviors and actions do.

Your colleagues may not always do everything as expected, but they all deserve to be treated with dignity, professionalism, and respect. Don't lower or dilute your expectations, but always approach customers and colleagues with the same respect and professionalism you would ask from them. Commit to following the golden rule: treat others as you would have them treat you. The golden rule still applies! Do unto others as you would have them do unto you.

You show respect—or lack of respect—in the way you approach someone, the way you communicate with individuals or a group, the way you make a person feel when he or she hasn't met expectations, and the process you use to make decisions. These are just a few of many actions and behaviors that determine your level of respect for those around you.

If comments from fellow colleagues and customers suggest you are not being true to your culture, it is vital to immediately examine your behaviors and attitudes. When your actions and behaviors don't match your stated values then your fellow colleagues and customers will question your true intentions. Leaders of excellence strive to be consistent in what they say and do. As the CEO of your position, you have to walk the walk.

At IEC, we frequently hear it said by organizational colleagues that "we manage and lead through praise and recognition and not fear and intimidation." Remember, a title does not define you—your behaviors and actions do.

You don't have to be perfect, but recognize that you're on a journey of continual improvement. Each of us is a work in progress, and as long we do not fall victim to ego and arrogance and instead yield to learning, we allow ourselves the opportunity to grow and improve.

In some organizations some leaders may be rude, disrespectful, mean, hurtful, and degrading to other team members during calls or in meetings. Feedback may come with words like "bullying," "loud," and "humiliating." Some leaders may gossip about other leaders, managers, and team members. Confidential and private information might be shared with those who should not be privy to that information. It doesn't matter if this is widespread or not; if even one, two, or three leaders do it, that is excessive. This must not be allowed in a culture of excellence!

Of course, it is difficult to be great and to do great; it's hard to strive for excellence at all times. Producing and exceeding expected results is tough! It is also difficult to observe and to tolerate colleagues who don't work hard, those who do not care, or those who do not seek to achieve at a high level. But it is not acceptable to blame and point fingers at others. It is never acceptable to treat colleagues with disrespect, to embarrass them, or to humiliate them for underperforming or for failing to meet expectations.

For a variety of reasons, some organizations operate in such a manner and support a top-down cultural architecture. The "higher-ups" need to prove that they are the bosses. They walk around, chests puffed out, putting a show on, making sure everyone knows who the bosses are.

In a culture of excellence, however, everyone already knows who the boss is; no one needs to prove it. The boss is the one supporting the team and each colleague, encouraging them, mentoring them, empowering them, trusting them, and engaging them! They are the primary motivators.

Imagine that a boss is introduced to a subordinate colleague's family at a company event. Rather than saying, "I'm Gary's boss," the leader of excellence says, "You must be so proud of Gary. We love him around here! We can always count on him giving us new ideas, helping others, and being a very positive example for us!"

There is no mention of who is boss and who is not. Imagine how that must make Gary feel! Imagine how his family must feel. It's that simple. That is how a leader of excellence embodies respect.

Always know and remember: the organization should act and behave as one. Also trust that no one is above it all; this conversation applies to the top level of the organization as well, where the leader should constantly be recalibrating so he or she is more and does more.

Time for some brutal honesty with yourself! Read, self-reflect, digest, and visualize the guidance below, and please be very mindful of how all of these matters apply to you.

The message here is that we must always be respectful and kind. We should not say things that are hurtful and we should not say things in a hurtful manner. We must not dilute our high expectations. Note that we don't ever want to imply that we should be weak. That is the furthest thing from our point here. But we must always honor the dignity of those around us. Everyone (and we mean everyone) deserves to be and must be respected at all times, regardless of their title, function, gender, race, ethnicity, age, sexual orientation, and national origin. Our titles and positions do not define us or separate leaders; our behaviors do. No one shows up to work to be disrespected, no matter what the circumstance. So let us all be mindful of how we behave and how we are perceived. Please trust that our colleagues watch our behaviors and actions at all times.

Acting with Courage

Leaders of excellence have the courage to take action to improve themselves and their teams and to exceed expectations as opposed to hoping, praying, and waiting for some outside force to prod them to get better! It takes courage to make mistakes and learn from them and become stronger. Leaders have the courage to authentically accept responsibility for all that goes wrong, and they certainly have the courage not to blame others and point fingers when issues and problems arise.

It is equally important that leaders have the courage to give credit to team members who go above and beyond to produce peak performance.

We can use our own experience at IEC as a case study in how leaders can act with courage in line with their values when facing difficult times. Every organization encounters periods of turmoil during change, whether it be an internal realignment or pressure from outside forces in the marketplace. IEC is no different in that respect. Change must take place in order for individuals, leaders, and organizations to properly evolve.

Several years ago, IEC went through a very difficult transition because of major, sweeping changes in the business and education sector. During this period of uncertainty, some IEC campuses had to slow down their operations until certain remediation could be developed. Although Dr. Fateri (IEC's CEO and one of the authors of this book) was not involved in the issue at the campus level, he later stood in front of several hundred colleagues at a company function and admitted that he "owned" the mistake. Dr. Fateri said it had taken place on his watch and that he'd let his colleagues down because he didn't forecast the changes. To this day, IEC colleagues still talk about the time Dr. Fateri owned the problem. He did not blame a campus; he did not blame a colleague; he did not blame a situation; he did not blame the sector; he did not point a finger at anything or anyone. The CEO completely owned the failure. All of it. He was humble. He made himself vulnerable. Out of that courageous act, Dr. Fateri earned the respect of every single colleague in the organization. That single act contributed greatly to the phenomenal culture of excellence colleagues of IEC still enjoy today.

Out of humility, out of vulnerability, out of honesty, comes courage. Comes strength. Comes respect. Comes honor.

As goes the leader, so goes the team. If you want a team of courageous men and women, model by being a courageous leader.

Understanding Kindness versus Weakness

Never mistake kindness for weakness! Leaders of excellence are courageous and charge forward with incredible vigor and zeal. They are positive, motivated, committed, and passionate!

Think about it. Everyone in the office knows who the boss is. Does the boss need to prove that he or she is the boss? In a culture of excellence, that is absolutely unnecessary. An organization of excellence operates with respect, for every single colleague seeks to honor what the boss asks the team members to do! That being said, when leaders have to make difficult decisions, they operate with respect and dignity for everyone involved. If, for example, leaders have to provide negative feedback to someone (no matter what level or in what situation), they aren't rude, demeaning, or dismissive, but they have to take care of business. They take care of business in a kind, respectful, and dignified manner.

In a culture of excellence, leaders encourage team members to be productive through praise, appreciation, and recognition—not through fear, intimidation, and bullying. And they ensure this value is upheld across teams, departments, and organizations. There are no exceptions. Leaders of excellence are always respectful and professional, and they expect the same of everyone else! No one should mistake kindness for weakness. Organizations of excellence have very high expectations for top performance, but they expect to achieve superior results through acceptable behaviors.

Let's look at an example to illustrate the point.

There is a job that must be accomplished, and it is on a tight timeline. Consider the approaches Supervisors #1 and #2 take to motivate Bob to get the job done.

Supervisor #1: "Bob, get this project done or I will write you up!"

Supervisor #2: "Bob, I know this is a huge project. We are all here to support you and you have resources at your disposal. What is it you need? As CEO of your position, I trust you will take charge of the project and let us know how to support you."

Which of these approaches will motivate Bob more? Which would motivate *you* more?

In both cases, it goes without saying that Bob needs to get the project done. In all likelihood, the supervisor will have to perform some kind of written counseling or guidance if the project is not finished. We can be pretty sure Bob is aware of that possibility, right? He is already under pressure to get this done.

Of course we all read this and hope Bob finished on time! But let's say Bob didn't.

For whatever reason, he didn't finish on time. Now what?

Yep. We have to provide written feedback. It is never easy to give critique; it's distasteful for many. But a leader of excellence knows it has to be done. Follow-through is necessary.

The good news is that it can be done in a respectful and constructive manner. If the supervisor has to create a write-up, he or she can do it with kindness, dignity, and respect.

The chances that Bob comes to work intending to fail are virtually nonexistent. We have yet to meet the colleague who comes to work and seeks failure. Bob will feel the failure even more if the write-up is confrontational and negative. Do we want Bob demoralized, or do we want him to learn from the mistake?

Are leaders of excellence top-down, negative bullies, or are they strong, encouraging, and kind?

Leaders do what must be done! They never

shirk their responsibilities, no matter how uncomfortable! But leaders of excellence always act in a dignified, respectful manner.

Always Be Consistent

We often say that the mother of excellence is consistency. All of us have enjoyed moments of greatness when we have achieved the extraordinary; it is truly an amazing feeling. But not many can consistently produce peak performance because that requires us to be at our best at all times—and that's hard even for the most worthy. Therefore, consistency is what separates good from great and ensures excellence. Chasing excellence is what strong leaders do. They exceed expectations consistently.

Many organizational leaders know how difficult it is to get to the Super Bowl. Only leaders of excellence know what it takes to repeat the Super Bowl time and time again.

Expressing Authenticity

Leaders of excellence understand that clear and continuous communication between manager and supervisor is critical to in order to establish an honest and fair professional relationship. When leaders are clear about expectations, they help their team members become accountable and push them toward becoming CEOs of their positions. Conversely, when leaders ignore and avoid direct and clear communication of expected results, they hurt team members' development, and the organization suffers. Know and trust that a culture of excellence doesn't recognize or promote a team member unless that team member has a history of exceeding expectation. Leaders must always help team members understand expectations and have an accurate awareness of their level of performance.

It's also vital to maintain authentic communication across the organization for a culture of excellence to flourish.

Examples of IEC enterprise-wide authentic communication include the following:

- State of the Company calls on a regular basis
- CEO "brown bag" lunch calls

- Leadership workshops and conferences
- Regular accountability meetings with the operations and executive teams
- Regular recognition programs and calls

There are many types of communication calls and meetings that take place in an organization of excellence. The point is to have them consistently and to ensure depth and content. The practices listed above are just a few examples among many possibilities that, when properly and consistently performed, will support a culture of excellence.

Types of Employees

An organization of excellence will typically have two types of employees with management/leadership titles:

- **Type 1**: Managers who are negative, unhappy, journalists, record keepers, historians, skeptics, spectators, cynics, brokers, critics, and powerless victims.
- **Type 2**: Managers who exhibit competitiveness, problem-solving ability, energy, tenacity, accountability, passion, fun, care, hard work, a sense of urgency, excellence, ownership, integrity, belief, and a hunger for peak performance.

Type 2 managers and leaders survive and excel in an organization of excellence. And type 1 managers and colleagues? Well, not so much.

Be honest with yourself. Which type are you? Ask your colleagues how they perceive you. Invite genuine feedback and critique.

Think about this for a minute: if you believe you have type 2 attributes but your boss doesn't support you, then you are in type 1.

If you have the courage and self-awareness to realize you have become a type 1 manager, someone who is a broker, a spectator, and a consultant, then it is time to recalibrate. If you catch yourself becoming cynical, negative, and skeptical, then you have work to do to become more self-aware. Perform deep self-assessment, and then get on with it! Get over yourself!

Ask yourself, *Am I doing well in quantitative results? Am I producing peak results with integrity and quality? Am I a great role model for the customers and colleagues around me? What am I doing to be part of the solution? What am I doing to significantly contribute to the greater good of my team, my department, my site, my store, my organization?* Should you truly want to grow as a manager and a leader, ask those around you to give you an objective assessment of you!

Whatever the results, understand the issue of cultural fit is not about who is good or bad—it doesn't matter who is right or wrong. Leadership excellence is all about serving customers with excellence and meeting expected results.

With this feedback in hand, design practices and routines to be the best type 2 leader of excellence you can be. Be truly and authentically accountable for your business. Take charge of your own destiny. Create greatness. Be an ambassador of excellence for every single customer and colleague around you! You are responsible for embodying these vitally important leadership behaviors and actions every single day. No stories, no excuses, and no fluff!

Being a leader of excellence, a superstar, a breakthrough leader, and the CEO of your position is all about how much you want to take charge of your life and your career. Are you strong enough to be accountable for your values and your performance? Do you understand the values required of a leader of excellence? And do you have what it takes to turn those values into action?

4

Putting Values
into Action

Putting Values into Action

Now that we've identified the values that make leaders of excellence, let's look at how they put that magic into action!

Surrounding Yourself with Top Talent

The first step to turning your values into action is to surround yourself with top talent. The highest priority is to have the right people on board in the first place. Too many companies don't understand that the success of the organization is not so much about policy or even about strategy; rather, successful and sustaining organizations have and maintain the right culture, and culture consists of like-minded people, not just people who need work. We are talking about people who understand a cause. We are talking about people who have passion, integrity, and the drive to be the best. These are people with a purpose. It's hard to execute your values if you're the only one upholding those standards.

Organizations of excellence recruit top talent for every role, team, and department across their enterprise. In his book *Good to Great,* Jim Collins suggests that good to great leaders, "first [get] the right people on the bus, (and the wrong people off the bus) and then figured out where to drive it" (Collins, 2001 p41.) It only makes sense, doesn't it? If we have a mediocre team, how can we expect exceptional outcomes? It just isn't possible!

For example, think of a sports team. Pick your favorite! If that team has mediocre talent, can we possibly expect them to win a championship series? To take a medal in the Olympics? Again, it just isn't possible! Winning championships takes the best of the best colleagues with talent and ability.

Organizations of excellence recruit top talent. They *require* it. They position themselves for success. They don't accept anything less, and neither should you!

It seems obvious that an organization of excellence requires the right kind of people to support it. An organization is only as good as the people in it. Hiring top talent should be an obsession for every leader, no matter their position or title! This is the first action leaders of excellence take to achieve objectives.

Leaders of excellence ask themselves the following questions:

- What am I doing to develop my team members?
- What am I doing to produce peak performance in every single aspect of the department so we can exceed expectations?
- What am I doing to improve the customer experience, the customer journey, and customer retention as well as all business measurements?
- What am I doing to ensure accurate customer feedback in each product or service?
- If it is a functional role, what am I doing to exceed the expectations of my customers in other departments or outside agencies?

Questions should also be geared toward uncovering empirical evidence of the organization's effectiveness! Remember, as CEO of your position, you own it—no matter what "it" is!

What Exactly Is Top Talent?

The term *top talent* may mean different things to different people. At the very core, a highly talented individual is a person with a demonstrable history of consistently achieving peak measurable performance in a specific area/department at a comparably sized organization offering similar programs, products, or services, and moving at the same or a higher pace.

A highly talented superstar is ambitious, competitive, and very hardworking. He or she is solutions-focused, accountable, tenacious, positive, hands-on, humble, and has a sense of urgency. Talented team members are passionate and committed to excellence, quality, industry compliance, and customer success.

It is not easy to find a team of such dedicated people! It can be difficult to find top talent: that's the reason we are igniting your obsession.

We promise it's not magic—it is leadership. But the first step is to face the brutal facts and then take deliberate and definitive steps to upgrade. If you realize you're not surrounded by top talent and your organization, productivity, and customer service suffer because of it, it's time to make a change.

Your customers deserve the best. It is your responsibility to provide it.

How Can You Ensure That You Have Top Talent?

Organizations of excellence are always searching for top talent and do not (and cannot) treat staff/management recruitment as an event. Good managers and supervisors should always be building a bench for every single position on the team. Organizations should upgrade and replace poor- and average-performing team members with talented professionals who have a history of peak performance. There should never be open positions, especially in areas critical to the management of the business.

Do you now have open positions on your team? Have you had areas and departments with poor, average, or below-average performance for months? Do you have poor performers on your teams and are you waiting, hoping, and praying for those team members to miraculously transform into superstars? Have you avoided facing the brutal fact that you have poor performers on your team?

Whether you're sweeping them under the rug or ignoring them altogether, it doesn't matter. Everyone around you will be aware that you have poor performers on your team, and that reflects badly on you as a leader. Recognize that accepting and dealing with poor performers is very difficult, but building a strong team is one of your top priorities as a leader.

Hiring top talent should be part of who you are. So transform this practice from an "event-driven" activity to an ongoing part of your culture.

How do you find top talent? How do you interview top talent?

Here are a few pointers to guide you:

1. Always be in charge of the search; do not delegate the responsibility to anyone else.

2. Have a committee on-site, at the store, region, department, and/or division level to review, discuss, and plan for searches for open positions.

3. Once the position is open, advertise it on LinkedIn, Indeed.com, and other recruiting sites. Ask colleagues to share your post to widen your network.

4. Email position openings to all internal contacts and ask for their referrals. For example, if you are in search of a production specialist, email all production specialists in the organization.

5. Using this method, you will generate

many resumes. If the position reports directly to you, review all resumes yourself. Remember, this is about accountability.

6. Set interviews as qualified resumes come in. Top talent candidates want to be treated with urgency, respect, and professionalism. Don't wait. Make the candidate feel important. Communicate with them on a regular basis.

7. When searching for top talent, review resumes for direct and relevant experience. Look for individuals who advance vertically within the same function. Do not search for potential; search for individuals who've been there and done that! Look for repetitive records of high achievement.

8. Always search for individuals who have been in the same organization for at least several years and have been promoted.

9. When hiring a manager for a department of ten, make certain the individual has experience managing at least ten individuals.

10. When searching for a direct report, make certain to call references. Speak with

people who have managed, worked alongside, and reported to the candidate. The objective here is to assess performance, productivity, and cultural fit. Did this person consistently meet/exceed expectations? Is this person a high achiever? Is this person accountable? Is this person a team builder? Is this person humble, hardworking, professional, and respectful? Is this person a winner?

11. When you have at least one or two top candidates, have a few others interview him/her, including subject-matter experts (vertical head) and other superstars in the organization with the same title (e.g., production specialist, production manager, etc.). This will provide a good opportunity to get the opinion of other leaders who know your culture and expectations of the organization.

12. Always recruit and hire talented people who will make you shine; you want team members who will make you proud.

Never settle!

This is a very important accountability issue. Your success depends on it. Don't hire underqualified team members! Searching for top talent is one of the most important responsibilities of a leader of excellence. Take it very seriously.

You are the CEO of your own position! Prove your accountability and commitment to excellence; be assertive, own it, and make hiring top talent a priority. It all starts with you!

With the right people on your bus, you can focus on pleasing your customers and achieving your strategic goals.

Communicating
Objectives of Excellence

Here is an interesting phenomenon you may have experienced. Some colleagues are surprised or shocked when confronted regarding their poor and unacceptable performance. In essence, your team members are surprised to learn that they are not meeting expectations!

How can this possibly be?

Let's examine your responsibilities first:

1. Do you clearly and repeatedly communicate your functional and behavioral expectations to your team members? Are you abundantly clear about what you expect from the different positions on your team?

2. Are you very clear about the behaviors you expect to observe daily? For example, do you explain it is important to be respectful, professional, on time, hardworking, and customer service-oriented? Do you explain it is important to respond quickly to email, requests, and calls?

3. Do you clearly communicate with your

team members when expectations are or are not met?

How are you doing on holding up your end of the bargain? You want to recognize your team members for meeting expectations, but you also want to be clear when team members fail to meet expectations. As with hiring top talent, coaching, developing, and providing constructive feedback to your colleagues should be a continuous process—not an event. Leaders of excellence support and encourage team members, helping them as much as possible. But there are times when team members must face the brutal facts about their performance, especially when they do not meet expectations. Remember, this is not personal; it's about commitment to your customers and focus on quality and achieving excellence. Please treat your team members as grown-ups; they deserve to be in the know. You owe your team members complete honesty, candor, and transparency. If they don't receive constructive feedback, they can't strive for excellence.

Organizations employ workers from multiple generations, from millennials to baby boomers to those from Generation X and Y. Each generation of colleagues brings various attributes, wishes, habits, perspectives, and demands. That's fantastic, as it allows for a diverse and fruitful community. However, please recognize that the organization itself must have one culture with one set of values; all colleagues, regardless of their history and background, must acculturate if they want to persist and succeed. Celebrate the diversity, but never compromise high expectations; standards for performance must remain constant at all times for every position.

Fardad Fateri & James E. York

An IEC Case Study

IEC acquired a set of several campuses on the East Coast in 2014, and the IEC leadership team quickly discovered that merging two cultures can be a very difficult and cumbersome process. No matter the best intentions of the two parties, the reality is there is an "acquirer" and an "acquiree." Inevitably, the acquiree feels like the forgotten member. In this case, there was also a significant geographical distance the company had to overcome (IEC headquarters is on the West Coast) as well as basic program and cultural differences. This is all very normal for a company merger, but that doesn't make it any less difficult, especially for the "acquiree."

The IEC leadership team knew that communication was key to successful integration. The company determined to send an "IEC cultural ambassador" to run a campus, to work with the new colleagues in order to help them understand and operate successfully within their new parent company's culture, and to hold "IEC culture workshops" in order to help the new colleagues assimilate to the very powerful, unique, and fast-moving culture of IEC.

By supporting one of the new campuses, the colleagues on the East Coast knew that the cultural ambassador was going through the same pain and challenges they were and could identify with them. The ambassador could also represent those challenges to the CEO and executive team, so IEC leadership could better understand the challenges faced by the newcomers. They spoke the same language.

The integration was a success! Over time, the new locations became acclimated to IEC's operating style and are now a set of highly energized, passionate, capable, and stable locations!

It is so critical to communicate frequently and keep everyone informed! There is no such thing as too much communication. Thinking, assuming, and wondering will lead to frustration, as it will hinder a leader's ability to be effective. So breakthrough leaders always ask, communicate, and share. They encourage team members to speak up and speak out. The only way leaders and teams can improve is to freely communicate their thoughts, insights, and observations. Leaders are only as good as their colleagues.

Equally as important is the timing of communication. When colleagues, employers, employees, and customers call or email, leaders of excellence respond quickly. You may not always have the correct answer, but you must always respond and inform the other party of the process and next steps. Ideally, a response should occur within one hour (that's TRUE breakthrough customer service), but no inquiry or request should go without a response for longer than twenty-four hours. This includes weekends! Remember, leaders of excellence make things happen, and this requires timely and effective communication!

What Is Timely Communication?

Let's look at an example to illustrate the point.

A supervisor is under pressure to get an annual year-end inventory completed. He is working with Mike, who is being very evasive and unresponsive in his communication with the supervisor.

Supervisor: "Mike, were you able to get the inventory completed? Did we receive all of the backlogged items we were expecting? This is year-end, and we have to have it done today. We're out of time."

Mike: "No, it's not done. I emailed one of the vendors three weeks ago and they haven't responded yet."

Supervisor: "Did you send a follow-up email? Did you try calling them? Did you ask one of your team members to stop by their office to check in with them?"

Mike: "No. They should have answered my email. I

guess we'll just have to note that item as a shortage on inventory."

At first glance, it appears that Mike is "on it" because he has an answer for everything. He has emailed the vendor. He blames the vendor for not responding. After all, isn't that the vendor's job? It becomes clear that the job just isn't going to get done.

But let's examine this exchange in a bit more depth. What else could Mike have done?

- If the email didn't get a response, send another one. And another one. And another one.
- Call the vendor every single day. Leave a voicemail message each time.
- Stop by the vendor's office (if local) and request the information.
- Escalate to the vendor's next-level supervisor.

- Tell his own supervisor of the issue, so his supervisor could help address it.
- Any number of other scenarios in which Mike OWNED the completion of the inventory.

The bottom line is that Mike did not act as the CEO of his position! He sent ONE email and expected someone else to own it. But it was *his* job to get it done.

What do you think Mike's answer should have been?

Right! Mike's answer should be: "You bet the inventory is done! One of the vendors was slow on getting back to me, so I called and emailed every day. I texted him and his staff. I stopped by his office on Saturday and was able to get the information I needed. Inventory is done. Next!"

A leader of excellence is relentless in following through, following up, and finishing, even if it takes emails, calls, or personal visits. Leaders get it done. They don't make excuses; they take ownership. They are accountable!

Be Sure to Prioritize

Every single day, we are faced with the questions of what we should focus on, what we should handle, and what we should achieve. These questions of priorities are amplified when there are only a few people in your area—even more so if you're the only one!

Let's explore some guidelines leaders can focus on to determine priorities and be CEOs of their position in a culture of excellence.

Assess the impact to the organization. For example, if you have to decide between working on an important policy on product integrity versus a dress code policy for your department, pick the policy on product integrity. Why? Because product integrity is critical; it applies to all of your customers and affects the quality of your office, site, department, and the entire organization! Dress codes are important, of course, but not nearly as important as product or service integrity.

By prioritizing large issues over smaller issues, you create more impact; always take care of larger issues because these involve more people. For example, improving a sales and finance department for a large site with more staff will have a greater impact on outcomes than working on a smaller issue, site, or department. Ideally, you want to focus on both but, if you cannot, pick the larger issue.

Have you heard of the 80/20 rule? Simply put, there are typically large issues in a department (20%) that, if properly addressed, will solve 80% of the problem(s) in that area.

While there are many methods of identifying and prioritizing issues, we might suggest displaying departmental issues on a Pareto chart. The Pareto chart allows you to identify the 20% that will provide a larger overall impact for your set of issues, regardless of the size of the site, department, or organization. Then attack the heavy hitters.

In our Figure A example, the top three heavy hitters are housing, transportation, and food. Solve the heavy hitter(s) and you solve the greatest impacting issues.

Figure A: Pareto Chart

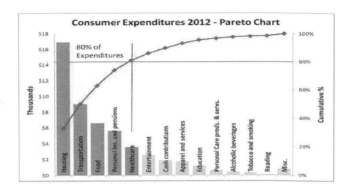

Available from: Bing Image Feed: http://www.bing.com/images/

Another important aspect of prioritizing is to select projects wisely. Always think big picture when investing your time and resources. Focus on what will create the greatest impact. At one point or another, you might have noticed several departments and numerous people working on a single project that makes up only a small percentage of your business. Every part of your business is important, no matter how small. But think about which efforts will make the greatest impact on the organization! Prioritize. These are the times when you have to outsource your trust and leverage talents at the site level.

Do not sweat the little stuff. And don't make something bigger than it is!

Only make decisions and focus on activities related to your organizational strategies and objectives. It makes no sense to worry about the overgrown trees in the employee parking lot if your customers are unhappy! And please don't try to convince others to worry about how those overgrown trees wither. Focus on your organization's strategies and objectives. Once you have achieved all objectives at expected levels, then allocate time to the overgrown trees.

The challenges you face are likely more complicated than the aforementioned scenario. But no matter the level, no matter the issue, no matter how complicated the problem seems, these basic principles work. If you're still unsure about how to prioritize, brainstorm with other leaders in your organization.

Remember, it is critical that leaders of excellence be wise and prudent with their time, energy, and priorities.

Focusing on Planning, Then Executing

We often get bogged down with hundreds of thoughts and activities, many of which may not actually matter. To combat this tendency, leaders must cultivate a results-focused culture.

The ideal approach to produce peak performance is to create thorough, thoughtful, comprehensive plans which are as detailed as possible. This makes execution more attainable and streamlined.

Of course, having a plan is important. An organization of excellence—a leader of excellence—must have a plan to guide the organization—the team—where they need to go. In essence, they must have a road map toward goal achievement—a road map toward success! For example, if we want to take our family on a vacation to Disneyland and we start our trip in New Jersey, we need a plan. We need to map our route! If not, we may very well start our trip in New Jersey, only to wind up in Canada! An effective organization must have a plan. Leaders of excellence have plans.

Once the plan is in place, leaders of excellence execute that plan! Leaders of excellence execute and produce expected results. Planning is done to ensure appropriate execution. Of course, we should always look for a well thought-out plan with details and contingencies, but it is the ability of the leader to execute that makes all the difference. Many organizations plan, and plan, and plan, and . . . plan . . . but the successful organizations understand that planning is but the initial step. The value of execution cannot be understated.

You may be working in a large organization. One of the benefits of large organizations is that you learn how to scale, standardize, and develop processes and plans. An unfortunate result, though, is you may lose that spirit of entrepreneurship that allows you to innovate and execute. Strive for a healthy balance between large organization planning and small organization execution. As a leader of excellence and as the CEO of your position, you are accountable not for producing the best plan but for attaining the best results that meet and exceed expectations. Therefore, next time you are invited to another call and another committee meeting, remember your objective is to execute and produce results. So during those meetings, keep your eye on the ultimate prize: *results*.

Be aggressive, do not accept "can't" as an answer; have a sense of urgency in all you do and execute ruthlessly to produce expected results.

Driving BHAGS

We have to give Jim Collins credit for this one! In his book *Built to Last*, Collins introduced the Big Hairy Audacious Goal (BHAG). Collins tells us that the BHAG (pronounced bee-hag) is a 'clear and compelling goal' (Collins & Porras, 1994/2002, p.94) for the organization that galvanizes the spirit of the organization. According to Collins, like the moon mission, "a true BHAG is clear and compelling and serves as a unifying focal point of effort, often creating immense team spirit. It has a clear finish line, so the organization can know when it has achieved the goal; people like to shoot for finish lines. A BHAG engages people; it reaches out and grabs them in the gut. It is tangible, energizing, and highly focused. People "get it" right away, and it takes little or no explanation."

And so it is with the organization of excellence. We operate under the principle of the BHAG. We live it and breathe it!

What does BHAG have to do with a culture of excellence?

A culture of excellence is built on potential, not on a budget! Merely achieving budget is failure to a leader of excellence—that signifies mediocre performance.

Many organizations build a budget and then play the "budget game" on how much they can get away with. "Under-promise and over-deliver" is a common mantra in many organizations. In an organization of excellence, however, the budget only serves as a minimum baseline. The target—the BIG HAIRY AUDACIOUS GOAL—in an organization of excellence is to drive the potential of the colleagues in the organization! There is no limit in an organization of excellence. Leaders of excellence only look at the budget as a set of numbers to completely demolish! Leaders of excellence add higher goals to a budget and then push to excel beyond those audacious goals!

Leaders of excellence never settle for "hitting the budget." Leaders of excellence laugh at the budget as we pass it by!

Years ago, during a strategic planning meeting, two members of an organization presented the "SuperPlan" to the CEO and his executive team. The SuperPlan was more than just a PowerPoint presentation with a set of numbers on a slide reviewing how the team would "hit budget." Not even close. The SuperPlan was a promise that these members would so far exceed their budget that there would be virtually no relationship between the budget and the actual outcomes. The BHAG was so outlandish, so far-fetched, that no one believed it. Except the CEO, that is. The CEO made the promise to the team that they would have everything they needed to achieve their goals. He told them that he believed in them. Sure enough, that team did achieve their SuperPlan goals that year! In fact, they over-promised and over-delivered by an extraordinary amount. And in doing so, the team acted as a catalyst for the entire organization to drive for higher results and take chances.

Don't Allow Bureaucracy to Get in the Way

Bureaucracy is a big problem for leaders of excellence. Even if your organization has various positions, titles, levels, and so forth, an organization of excellence must act and behave as a flat organization. Don't lose those features of entrepreneurship that allow you to get things done—done well and on time.

If supplies or products are in the storage room, your team should put them on the shelves for the customers to see! Who are you waiting for?

If a customer seems lost in your lobby, stop and help him or her.

If a department needs help, go help them!

It doesn't matter if you occupy the most powerful position in the company. Don't become a prisoner or a victim of your titles and positions! Get things done. Be empowered to meet expectations. No stories, no excuses, no fluff.

Trusting Your Superstars

If you are an executive or a member of a corporate staff, it is important to note that you have many superstars in your offices, in your sites, at your facilities, at your stores. They are just as good as you are! Being part of an executive team or corporate staff or having a higher title does not necessarily make you better! Trust your team members at your locations and empower them to make decisions and get the work done.

In most organizations, a very high percentage of your resources are in the field for the right reason—because that's where your customers are. Recognize that benefit and learn to use these resources intelligently.

Collaborate and work as a team. This concept of acting as one is difficult for many people to digest, but it is a critical paradigm to work toward. It is important to remember that all colleagues make up one organization. There is no "us and them"; it is just "us." To the outside world; to customers, to vendors, to employers, the organization of excellence appears as one organization. Our customers don't know (or care) what department a colleague might be in; therefore, any unfavorable inaction and misbehavior is a reflection on the entire organization. Don't let ego, pride, or petty jealousy get in the way of building the strongest team, department, and organization. This is only possible when you empower your superstars to do their best work and then trust them to do it.

Furthermore, it doesn't matter what department you are in! Work is divided by departments to achieve order, ensure maximize efficiency, and create discipline. Therefore, regardless of what title you have and what department you are in, you must do all that is necessary within acceptable operations as well as regulatory frameworks to support your colleagues at every level. In essence, leaders of excellence are accountable for making their colleagues successful and their customers satisfied. In the culture of excellence, employees are one, and they must act accordingly.

At IEC, we are structured into what we identify as four different areas:

1. Admissions, which builds the value of education
2. Financial services, which provides finance options for access to education

3. Education, which delivers the value of education
4. Career services, which delivers the promise to help our students build a future they can be proud of

At IEC we view our admissions and financial aid areas as "one team" in spite of the "separation of duties" between the two teams. Although they have different functions, their ability to work together is vital to serve the customer (our students). Both teams are equally accountable for common results. Their mantra became *One team one mission*. Results improved dramatically and were evident in overall customer satisfaction and organizational outcomes.

Always Focusing on Solutions

From the time we are young children, we are socialized to see what's wrong with the world around us and to identify the person(s) who caused the problem. Identifying problems in organizations is terribly important. But finding solutions and solving problems doesn't stop there. What is much more important and significantly more difficult is finding thoughtful solutions to problems.

How do leaders of excellence facilitate this process? Simple! They use a solutions-focused approach. You may not be accustomed to gathering quantitative evidence, identifying and understanding the problem, and then developing and executing robust and creative solutions to produce expected results, but this is the most effective approach to finding and executing solutions. This is an essential skill for leaders of excellence. Having problems is not necessarily a bad thing—it's the nature of life on this planet and a normal part of every professional's job—but not having viable solutions creates negativity, dogma, and stagnation. One significant attribute that separates ordinary employees from CEOs of their position is the ability to solve difficult problems and exceed expectations.

Leaders will always face challenges both large and small regardless of their role or level in the organization. Organizations will always face challenges as well. But these challenges create opportunities for team development, professional growth, and personal mastery. Leaders must face the brutal facts and be deliberate in regard to their attitudes, behaviors, and actions. Most importantly, leaders of excellence look within and make changes to themselves and their performance before asking their colleagues to change. Leadership titles do NOT exempt a person from living organizational values; in fact, your title makes you a role model for others, responsible to do more and be more. In other words, you have to be the change you want to see in the team members around you.

Keeping Your Focus on Customer Service

One of the most powerful tools all organizations can access is right in their hands: access to the customer. Organizations of excellence ask their customers what satisfies them! Ask the customer how you can provide excellence and then go about providing it! A customer survey is an extraordinary tool that will allow you to do just that. Surveys help us (and our customers) identify what our customer needs and wants, and if we listen to the customer, we have our very own road to success! We are in essence asking them to tell us how to be great! So, let's be great!

Think about the 80/20 rule. If you gather data from the customer and put the information into the Figure A Pareto (http://www.bing.com/images/) analysis, there you have it! Start by satisfying the larger items so you can positively impact the majority of your customers and then work down the line to create greatness by going the extra mile. Work all the way down until you solve the smallest issues possible.

Customer service is arguably one of the most misunderstood terms. Providing customers with breakthrough customer service doesn't mean you have to give them everything they want! In most businesses, there are multiple expectations for several different customers, both internal and external.

All customers must be treated with urgency, respect, dignity, kindness, courtesy, professionalism, passion, and care. The same behavior holds true with colleagues, employers, and outside organizations. Remember that your customers can always choose to go to another business for their needs. What will set you apart is all that you do to make your customers feel needed, wanted, and special. We have to always, always meet and preferably exceed customer expectations. Plan to treat your customers with excellent customer service at all times.

A culture of excellence strives to support leaders of excellence in all possible ways. Just as we ask customers what they need and then go about satisfying those needs, so must we approach our superstar staff. We must know what they need in order to be successful! These are our CEO superstars! We must give them the tools they need!

Supporting teams in the field and on the production line is vital, as is customer facing.

We must provide all internal customers

with customer service excellence. This means that we must exceed the expectations of each and every customer every day. Probably the easiest example is responding to emails, texts, and phone messages in a timely manner. This means within minutes when possible, hours when not. You might have read through threads of emails showing many managers and team members not responding to key questions and requests from customers for days; that is unacceptable. And forwarding an email to a colleague for further action does not exempt us from our obligation to respond. These are the most basic tenets of customer service—you understand the point!

So let us ask you! Are you exceeding the expectations of your customers, your team members, and your colleagues in other departments, sites and locations?

Seek First to Understand

Habit five of Stephen Covey's *The 7 Habits of Highly Effective People* advises, "Seek First to Understand, then to be Understood" (Covey, 2004, p247.). Simply put, focus on hearing rather than on being heard. How often are you thinking about what you'll say in a conversation rather than listening to what the other person is saying? Listen to understand! What is the customer or team member trying to tell us? What is their point of view? According to Covey, "Communication is the most important skill in life. You spend years learning how to read and write and years learning how to speak. But what about listening? What training have you had that enables you to listen so you really, deeply understand another human being from that individual's own frame of reference?" (Covey, 2004 p.249).

Furthermore, Covey suggests that, "The key is to genuinely seek the welfare of the individual, to listen with empathy, to let the person get to the problem and the solution at his own pace and time. Layer upon layer—it's like peeling an onion until you get to the soft inner core." (Covey, 1989/2004 p. 263)

How much better will your colleague feel

. . . how much better will your spouse, significant other, children . . . even friends feel when you actively listen to understand? Give them the gift of your time . . . the gift of your genuine *intent to understand*. Many problems in the world could be solved with this small but very powerful concept.

For example—how does it feel when you enter someone's office, or you are at a retail establishment, and the person you expect to serve you doesn't truly listen to what you need? What if they continued looking at their computer and don't even turn to face you? What if they continue talking to the other person behind the counter rather than asking you . . . and paying attention to . . . what *you* need? Although these seem like very small things, the message they present is enormous. What is your response when someone approaches you? Do you stop what you are doing and listen?

Leaders of excellence listen with the intent to understand! Don't listen merely to formulate your own response. After all, don't you want to know the truth? If you are a lifelong student, you'll have the courage to listen and learn.

Leaders of excellence are lifelong learners!

Always Seeking to Learn

As leaders of excellence, when we visit different stores, locations, plants, facilities, and so forth, we should always seek to learn a great deal from people at "ground level." Treat these visits as opportunities to get a wider view of your organization's reach. It is important that we let our teams know that we will not give up until we all create and sustain a fantastic organization and become a premier provider of goods, products, or services in our respective businesses.

Consistent with our quest to achieve greatness in all we do, we all have to know a great deal about all that is going on around us. Therefore, we can ask ourselves, "How much do we know about what we do individually and collectively on-site, regionally, and/or divisionally? Whether you are a CEO, a vice-president, a divisional leader, a site supervisor, a production worker, a clerical worker—it doesn't matter! In a well-functioning organization where each colleague is the CEO of their position, every colleague matters.

We need to be familiar with the measurable expectations of all that we do, and we must be familiar with the roles and responsibilities of our positions.

Furthermore, in an organization that promotes communication and shared understanding, employees should be informed and know about other departments' performances and achievements.

It is so very important to let our teams know that we also want to learn from *them*. In many cases (perhaps even in most cases), team members will be experts in what they do. We *should* learn from them!

Visiting locations also lets leaders of excellence assess the talent in the field. We get to see colleagues in action rather than on a conference call or on a report somewhere. Visiting locations lets us see the magic as it happens! It lets us in on their world! The real world—not a cubicle at a headquarters office!

When we visit locations, we can ask our field experts what they do, how they do it, when they do it, and with whom they do it. No one in the organization is the expert of everything. We all must learn and experience together. As one unit.

When we visit campuses, we can learn a few things by asking the right questions. If we truly want to learn as well as to assess the talent in the field, we can seek to understand the knowledge and commitment of the colleagues doing the work.

Some key questions to ask your team might be:

1. Do you "really" know what the expectations are for you and your department?
2. What are your roles and responsibilities?
3. How do you know when you are successful?
4. Do you know when your department is successful?
5. Do you know when your site is successful?
6. Do you know what success looks like for your region?
7. Do you know the numerical requirements of your role? Your department? Your region? What should it be?
8. How many employees do you have on your site? In your office?
9. Do you know what your colleagues in other departments "really" do?
10. Do you fully understand the relationship and interdependencies between all departments?
11. Do you know the expectations of your colleagues in other departments?
12. What do you know about your organization?

13. Do you know the vision and mission of your organization?

14. What is your role in making your department, your site, your office, your division, your organization successful?

15. What is your responsibility in making sure your customers are successful?

16. What does quality mean to you? What does quality mean to your department and to your role?

17. What does superior customer service mean to you, to your department, and to your office?

18. What does "greatness" mean to you, to your department, and to your office? Your company?

19. What does top performance mean to you, to your department, and to your office?

If your organization wants to achieve excellence, to meet and exceed business goals, and to be first in class in your community, all employees must have a shared understanding of individual and collective responsibilities. It is the responsibility of leaders of excellence to ask themselves the tough questions and to seek answers to those questions—to learn.

The aforementioned discussion and associated questions are for every single member of the organization to address, especially you as a leader of excellence. It is perfectly okay to not have answers to one or more of the above questions, but it is not okay to ignore the questions altogether. Leaders have a responsibility to find answers to these questions. Go to your colleagues and ask and seek necessary answers! Take an active role in being a significant part of the solution in building your business. Be the CEO of your position. Take charge. Create your destiny. When every member of the organization takes such initiative, it's inevitable that you'll achieve your objective of building a world-class organization!

Holding Regular One-on-One
Steering Meetings

Though you may attend all kinds of meetings during the course of your weekly duties in regard to operations, because of the size and focus there is little time to go deep with any one particular coworker.

Consider establishing one-on-one meetings to influence, mentor, and steer influential colleagues on your team. It doesn't matter what level or position this colleague holds; choose people of influence or those who would benefit from your influence.

One-on-one meetings can be very powerful when you and your colleague sit down in private, face-to-face, and just talk. Ask your colleagues how they're doing. Ask how their family is. Ask how things are going at work. Be authentic. Be genuine. Open the floor for discussion. Be sure to actively listen to their concerns, their issues, and their feelings so you can help steer, direct, or influence them when necessary. Always be thinking of how you can support the colleague's success.

In one-on-one meetings, you establish relationships with your colleagues that allow for trust, honesty, and rapport. They get the sense that you honestly care. They feel they have a direct line to you. How powerful is that?

You can influence even the most difficult situations by mentoring your colleagues. But mentoring colleagues means you need to take the time to meet with them, to invest in them. These must be high-priority meetings, not the kind you just cancel because there is "too much going on right now."

One-on-one meetings are a prime way of influencing colleagues' adaptability to organizational culture. These meetings don't always have to be with direct reports—you can meet with anyone on your team: directors, associate directors, department leads, supervisors, lead employees, line employees—the position doesn't matter. It is the person . . . the colleague . . . the customer . . . that matters!

As you direct, influence, and mentor a colleague in the direction they should go, you may find that many "communication problems" you had with this person previously fade over time. With deeper relationships comes greater communication.

Asking Yourself the Tough Questions

As leaders of excellence, it is vital that we don't fool ourselves. "You can fool some of the people some of the time, but you can't fool all of the people all of the time." Every heard of that saying? Let's just break it down into something meaningful. Let's cut right to the chase. At the end of the day, what good does it do to try to fool anyone, much less ourselves? Why not deal in truth? Why not deal with the "brutal facts," even if they are about ourselves or our teams? Leadership requires character. Character is built through honest assessment.

Helpful questions might include the following:

1. Do I have the right talent on my team?
2. What have I done to make sure I have the best players on my team?
3. How many team members have I developed to perform at expected levels?
4. Have results in my area improved this week, this month, this quarter, and this year?
5. How would I rate my own productivity and performance as compared to expectations,

as compared to the best version of ME, and as compared to the best version of my business?

6. If I am meeting or exceeding expectations, what am I doing to ensure I continue to overachieve? If I am NOT meeting expectations, what significant actions am I taking to change the unsuccessful path I am on?

7. With all that I have done, what have been my measurable achievements in the past week, month, quarter, and year?

Remember, when you decide to excel: waiting, hoping, and praying, although therapeutic, won't help! You have to act with vigor, tenacity, grit, and conviction. Also understand that excellence and greatness aren't just pie-in-the-sky dreams; they are achievable for leaders of excellence every single day.

Positive Messaging

To our executive readers: organizations spend a lot of time and money on building their brand! But nothing builds your brand more effectively than your behaviors and actions as executives in the organization! As vertical heads and top operations executives, what you say and how you say it, what you do and how you do it, how you behave and how you treat others define you individually and collectively. Who you are and what you do define you as an organization because your team members emulate your behaviors—and then it all cascades to the front line. So what your customers experience is a reflection of who and what you are as executives. Indirectly and directly, you touch everyone in this organization.

The objective of staff and the executive team is to support an organization that has very high expectations; one that is always focused, disciplined, ambitious, accountable, and compassionate.

How do you achieve your objectives and develop a brand that would truly be the envy of your industry?

Although some of the following comments might seem a bit elementary, it's the basics that count the most. Many organizations avoid and ignore these basic but critical issues, but these are the very topics that separate good from great organizations. As an organization grows, it is vital that its values remain constant. From the top to the bottom of the organization, employees must be focused on achieving objectives while remaining true to core values.

1. Do not share confidential information with your team members, colleagues in other departments, and/or friends outside of your organization. If in doubt, ask your superior what is confidential.

2. Do not share your dissatisfaction or unhappiness about something or someone that is bothering you with colleagues in your department, other organizational colleagues, or colleagues outside of your organization. Instead, speak with your superior or confront the person who is causing the problem. Leaders speak up and speak out. Regardless, venting to others, although innocent, projects a negative image of YOU and your leadership team.

3. Do not listen to rumors, and stop them

when you hear them. This should go without saying, but never spread rumors to others inside or outside of your organization. When you engage in such discourse, it reflects poorly on you as an individual. Worse, it reflects poorly on your organization, all the way up to your executive team. We do not want our internal or external colleagues to think our executives lack organizational tact, maturity, and sophistication.

4. Do not share negative feelings, emotions, or information on social media, either directly or indirectly. Remember, you are a leader, and what you say negatively influences people's perception of you and your organization. Also know that internal colleagues, industry vendors, and external colleagues view what you write on social media, so if you don't have any positive news, feelings, behaviors, or actions to share about your team or organization, refrain from posting about them. Again, leaders confront issues head on. If you have a problem, speak with your manager or the person responsible for the conflict.

5. Be disciplined! Discipline separates the organization of excellence from other organizations. Focus on your vision and strategies at all times. Leaders of excellence understand that discipline achieves expected results and supports your organization's strategies and annual objectives. Everything you do should focus on your annual objectives in support of your strategies. Your discipline and focus will then cascade to other levels of the organization. Exhibit and manifest behaviors associated with disciplined individuals and organizations.

Be sensitive to site priorities and expectations. It's really that simple.

The objective as members of staff is to support, guide, and partner with your colleagues at the "boots on the ground" levels to meet and exceed expectations in line with your strategies and annual objectives. Be sensitive to the following:

- Key customer dates
- The how and not always the what

- Calls and training sessions based on what is good for your colleagues
- Owning the outcomes
- The fact that site success is your success
- Being an action leader

Key customer dates. Don't have conference calls with local sites on key customer dates, as they will be busy serving customers. For example, when you are setting up a trip to visit a field location, double-check your calendar. Compare it with colleagues' calendars so you aren't all addressing the same issue from different locations or in different venues. Double-check to ensure your work is fruitful and meaningful. Then, when you perform the activity, get right down to doing the work. Help, train, show, and demonstrate how work gets done. Your top staff members will be those who help colleagues achieve expectations.

Focus on the "how" and not always the "what." The how might be the methodology of your approach. Is it compliant? Is it effective? Is your communication thorough? Respectful? Does it include those who need to know? How will information be communicated to others? How will I execute this quickly and efficiently?

Then, focus on the what. What procedures need to be followed? What processes need to take place? What information will be critical to those involved? What hours will the team need to work? Always confirm that your colleagues fully understand expectations and what needs to happen. The foundation must be confirmed. It's the *how* part that separates colleagues in the organization from one another.

Organize and plan calls and training sessions. These should be based on what is good for your colleagues at the site level, not what is good for you. Remember, your responsibility is to serve your colleagues and help them achieve expectations.

Own the outcomes. Own outcomes at the same level of accountability as your colleagues at the site level so you can partner with them in finding solutions and executing plans to meet expectations. Your staff members who "own" expectations are respected the most because they are known to care just as much.

Site success is your success. Therefore, when your colleagues at the store level, the site level, or the department level are successful, you'll be successful. Plan your entire strategy and actions around this concept.

Be an action leader. Don't be a broker or consultant. Colleagues at the store level, site level, and the department level will appreciate advice, but they love those who can partner with them and get the work done to achieve expected results!

Remember, waiting, hoping, and praying will not enhance your team's ability! You have to take swift and definitive action to improve your team's strength. Do not be fearful of the attrition of poor or average performing team members, but do fear the attrition of your superstars who carry your department, your stores, and your organization.

Catching People in the Act of Doing Something Right

If you are in a position of support or oversight for a number of employees, locations, stores, regions, and so forth, maintain respect and dignity as you visit different colleagues and locations. Don't be overly critical, trying to find out "what is wrong" with that location. In fact, focus on what is RIGHT with that location! Of course, you always provide direct, honest, and authentic feedback, but make sure your tone is supportive. Encourage and praise your employees for things they're doing right. That positive reinforcement goes a long way.

Let's look at an example to illustrate the point. Supervisor #1 and Supervisor #2 are giving feedback to Susan regarding some challenges facing her production team.

Supervisor #1: "Susan, your production team is doing it all wrong. I thought we told you the process was changed two weeks ago! Why do I have to come here to tell you that you're doing it wrong? Don't you listen on our conference calls?"

Supervisor #2: "Thank you for spending time with us today, Susan. We are very impressed with several components of your operation! The way you reduced the number of steps in the process from ten to seven really helps increase efficiency! There are a couple of areas that need to be updated, though, so let's talk about those. We must not have communicated the changes properly. What else can we do to help you?"

Which would you be more likely to accept, appreciate, and make adjustments for? Which makes you feel more supported?

It's certainly okay to provide feedback on what is wrong. But it's essential to provide feedback on what is right! Catching people in the act of doing something right doesn't mean you have to couple it with something they are doing wrong. It is even better when you catch people in the act of doing something right and then you let them know. Imagine how motivating that is for your colleagues!

Keeping an Eye on the Financials

Leaders of excellence actively manage their financial budget.

Not all of us are born with a calculator-type brain. Not all of us enjoy running the numbers. But leaders of excellence learn to use historic report data and results in order to make meaningful changes in operations. For example, if your location is growing but you spend more money than you bring in then the funds aren't being used properly. Or perhaps you spend according to budget, but you don't grow according to budget. In that case, the funds still aren't being used properly. Leaders must be able to manage funds and track finances so expenses and revenue are in line with one another to meet expectations. If your outcomes are not in line with expectations, you need to make a change to your expenses. If working with financials is difficult then take charge! Find experts in your organization who can help you master the art of managing finances!

Watching the bucks means more than saving money. Being judicious with expenditures also sends a message of value to those around you. Colleagues look to leaders of excellence, watching their behavior closely; they'll notice if you are modeling the values you espouse as CEO of your position.

Often, being fiscally responsible simply involves a little extra time, effort, and good thinking.

Consider the following IEC example as a case study.

An IEC campus leader noted that the chairs in an office were bought eight or nine years ago and were starting to fall apart. The leader's immediate reaction was to replace them. However, upon visiting his students' classrooms, he noticed that the chairs used by students, our customers, needed upgrading. The campus leader put his own office chairs on hold in order to better serve the customer, even though that particular campus was significantly below the expense budget.

Leaders of excellence should cut expenses when necessary and be prudent with their spending, but they can also build by making the right investments in the right areas. Don't shy away from discussing finances with your team; set the tone and play a significant role in only spending where necessary, which includes not spending on unnecessary luxuries.

In this example, the campus staff and customers saw that the leader was following through with what he said he believed in—taking care of the team and the customers first. Staff began to feel more excited about new chairs and basic supplies. They felt heard; their boss was listening.

Being the CEO of your position; making the right choices; and keeping the team focused on how they can improve, execute, and achieve objectives is primary. Therefore, reducing any distractions—like the team not having the tools to succeed—is management's responsibility. Leading by example and doing what is right are values that make an immediate impact on morale and performance.

Leaders of excellence are resourceful, they ensure the efficient use of materials, and they prioritize spending in areas that enhance the customer experience.

Driving Results through Strategic Focus

In a culture of excellence, team members know what is important and what to focus on. Leaders of excellence understand that what we focus on will get the attention it needs.

Leaders of excellence understand the Hawthorne effect.

The Hawthorne effect is a psychological phenomenon that produces an improvement in human behavior or performance as a result of increased attention from superiors, clients, or colleagues (Daniel & Rouse, 2018).

The Hawthorne effect was first seen in the 1920s at Western Electric Company's Hawthorne Works, from which the term is derived. The Hawthorne studies were designed to find ways to increase worker productivity. Increasing the amount of light in the workplace had a measurable positive effect on employee productivity. However, the researchers also found that when they lowered the lighting levels, productivity still increased. In fact, for a limited period after any change in the illumination level, the workers' average output increased. The researchers concluded that the specific conditions tested for had nothing to do with the productivity increases (Daniel & Rouse, 2018).

What does this mean to us? The simple act of being observed made productivity increase. As simple as that! Of course, in different organizations this concept can take place differently, but the important thing to remember is that when we focus on things, they change. When we pay attention to our colleagues, to processes, to issues, they change. It is then up to us to decide HOW we can handle it as leaders of excellence to make sure these changes work toward our organizational goals.

Organizations of excellence understand the fact that what they focus on changes. As can be observed in the Hawthorne effect (Daniel & Rouse, 2018), when we focus on the important things, they change by the mere fact that we are focusing on them. You don't have to be condescending, mean, or negative. You can be respectful, understanding, and direct. The leader's job is to focus on things that are important to the organization.

What you focus on is what you change.

Running an organization requires focus on many, many areas. It requires a balance of several indices, all of which are important. At IEC, we know that as one area becomes unbalanced, we must focus on it—we make it public, we track it. And the outcome increases! It's all about putting focus, expectations, and accountability on the areas that need it.

As in the case of setting our own BHAGs, once we make our target goals public, our teams know that we have to focus specifically on them in order to achieve them. We cannot allow ourselves to be distracted from those goals! This is key to organizational success. Leaders of excellence understand this concept, and they don't waste time on minor distractions.

Focus on it and you will achieve it!

And so you have it! What we focus on changes.

Wrapping Up

Hopefully our time spent together has been meaningful for you. It certainly has for us! You now have a "quiver" of "leadership excellence arrows" with which to operate. Do other organizations operate with their own culture, their own quiver of arrows? Of course they do! But is it as well defined? Perhaps not. Our message to you is that it is vital to establish a "leadership excellence precedence" in your organization—or even just for yourself—in order to be productive, successful, and happy in whatever you do as your vocation.

At the beginning of the book, Dr. Fateri indicated that he came upon IEC during his search for purpose. So it is with James York, coauthor, as well as many of the colleagues within the organization. We have found something we love—somewhere we fit. It involves extraordinary self-awareness, extraordinary commitment. Extraordinary effort. But for us, all of this has meaning. Our own purpose has been fulfilled.

And so it can be with you! Just find (or create!) the right organization—the thinking organization that commits its ideals on paper; an organization that involves colleagues in the development of a very special, very powerful, very meaningful experience. An organization that understands the importance of honesty, respect, and dignity.

At IEC, we have a saying. "Culture Eats Strategy for Lunch." This statement is typically attributed to behaviorist Peter Drucker (1982); however, we can all learn the importance of this lesson. If we don't have a culture we can believe in, a culture that drives powerful principles and concepts, then no matter how much we talk and talk and talk about our "strategy," it simply won't happen without a distinctive and well-defined foundation of culture.

You might be wondering which principle in the book is most important. The truth is that while we have certainly reviewed many concepts and principles in our time together (and each one can arguably be the most important one), the litmus test is how you determine to act, to lead, and to look at and accept the brutal facts. Your organization will undoubtedly be a bit different than IEC. Of course! That is as it should be. But the principles and concepts we talk about are universal in nature. They apply across the board, no matter what organization you belong to or what you do within that organization.

Consider these concepts and principles as an umbrella—a set of constructs under which you operate. They become the "way you do business." You can operate with dignity, respect, honesty, kindness, and the other concepts in the book and be effective, efficient, impactful, and successful!

We wish you well!

Epilogue

Organizational culture is the single most important determinant of organizational success over a long period of time. In addition, organizational culture is the most significant factor in setting one organization apart from and above others. There are many articles and interviews that feature leaders of successful organizations discussing the stellar performances of extraordinary organizations, and more often than not they mention hard work, unique business theses, innovative product ideas, luck, and other similar factors as reasons for the organizations' success. These may be true, but they're not at the heart of organizational success—they're merely symptoms of that success. The fire that ignites hard work, innovation, passion, vigor, competitiveness, and accountability is *organizational culture*. All values and attributes of top-performing organizations are emerging properties of organizational culture.

In this book, we've shared with you many

thoughts, insights, observations, practices, and experiences that are all emerging properties of the culture we've deliberately built at International Education Corporation (IEC) to produce peak performance. This culture was developed to help the organization sustain viability during periods of turbulence, uncertainty, and trouble. Every organization has a culture. Some organizations are cognizant of their values, and they work hard to uphold them to promote greatness, while other organizations are completely unaware of who they are. Organizational culture develops whether it is deliberate or not. Organizations that sustain greatness over long periods of time have values that are shared by all team members. This is the secret to our success at IEC. Members of the IEC community all share the same values, and this has helped the organization sustain greatness through good times and bad.

It is hard to describe culture in motion, as the feelings and emotions are better felt than described. However, we've done our best to explain the great values that have allowed IEC and many other organizations to survive and prosper. The values that make up an organization's culture also empower individual team members to feel needed, to know they are important, and to believe that they matter. People want to work for an organization that values their contribution, an organization that allows them to make a meaningful difference, an organization that recognizes excellence. Everyone wants to work for an organization he or she can be proud of, so leveraging that desire helps develop amazing culture. However, on the flip side, not fueling a person's pride at work will inevitably build a culture anchored in cynicism, dogma, stagnation, and skepticism.

Leaders of excellence spend ample time focusing on values that develop stellar culture because they know products, ideas, strategies, plans, and highly paid executives don't create greatness: *culture* produces greatness. This is the lesson we've learned at IEC. This is the lesson all leaders learn when they experience breakthroughs in organizations; culture creates greatness.

While the concepts, examples, and explanations of values in the preceding chapters are specific to our experience at IEC, these ideas will have the same impact on any organization, whether it is a small private company or a large nonprofit public organization. With proper leadership, organizational culture can be created in any organization so as to produce peak performance and ensure productivity.

It is important to note that the concepts explained in this book also apply to individuals at a personal level. Each person has the capacity to be fully accountable, to have vigor, intensity, passion, and to be the CEO of his or her position and life. Individuals do not have to wait for someone else to guide them. When applied professionally and personally, the attributes, skill sets, values, and concepts discussed in this book will have a powerful impact on a person's career and personal life.

Our ambition in writing this book was to create a platform for all organizations and individuals to take a personal role in creating their own destinies. We hoped to demonstrate it is possible for anyone to become the architect of their own future. Most importantly, we wanted to encourage every reader to become an active participant in shaping their own life. If I can do it—if we can do it—anyone can do it. But you must believe. You must take personal responsibility. You must push through all obstacles, barriers, and negativity to test your capacity and to become the best version of yourself.

Theorists have varied definitions of organizational culture and different opinions regarding the role excellence plays in organizational culture. But for the most part, theorists take a very academic approach to defining and making attributions to cultural excellence. Academicians, organizational anthropologists, and business theorists have created sophisticated and thoughtful models depicting excellence in organizational culture. Organizations that have a clearly articulated mission, vision, and values statement are expected to achieve excellence in organizational culture.

Our approach to the subject has been more unorthodox by comparison. Although we share a strong academic background, we deliberately took a nonacademic practitioner-focused approach in describing a culture of excellence because we wanted to demonstrate how ordinary people create extraordinary cultures. We wanted to show you how employees with passion, ambition, vigor, trust, accountability, humility, imagination, respect, and love can create a culture of excellence by sharing the same values. We wrote this book for ordinary people and for practitioners because we wanted this book to be useful. We hope this book will do more than just collect dust on a shelf alongside hundreds of other books on leadership and organizational culture. We hope you'll use it on your journey to excellence. To your success!

References

Bing Image Feed. Pareto Chart. https://binged.
it/2yo6KlZ

Collins, J. *Good to Great,* New York: HarperCollins
Publisher, 2001

Collins, James C., and Porras, Jerry I. *Built to
Last,* New York: HarperCollins Publishers,
1994/1997/2002.

Covey, Stephen R. *The 7 Habits of Highly Effective
People.* New York:

Fireside Book by Simon & Schuster, 1989/2004.

Daniel, Dianne, and Rouse, Margaret. *Hawthorne
Effect.* Retrieved May 26, 2018. http://whatis.
techtarget.com/definition/Hawthorne-effect

Drucker, Peter F. *The Practice of Management.* New
York: HarperCollins Publishers, 1982.

Merriam-Webster, s.v. "culture," accessed April 10,
2018, https://www.merriam-webster.com/
dictionary/culture.

Appendix A

We the People of IEC

IEC has a magical culture! We have created a culture which most practitioners read about in text books and case studies. An organization's culture goes to the very heart of its identity and the very essence of its existence. I never felt so strongly about the strength of an organization's culture to take a deliberate approach to protect it and leverage it for the viability of our future as one of the best career education companies in the country. But I feel very strongly about our culture at IEC and its contribution to whom we are and who we must remain to produce and sustain top results in the future.

Although words cannot authentically capture and describe the true essence of our culture, the following are the collective attributes, values, and behaviors we exhibit at IEC. None of these behaviors are independent of one another and in fact they are inter-related, co-dependent, and it is their direct collective connectivity that creates our unique identity and our extraordinary culture. I ask that you share this document with your colleagues, discuss it regularly and make it a critical part of your work life every day.

- We lead through Recognition, Gratitude, Appreciation, Praise and Inspiration
- We have heart
- We love to serve
- We manage and lead by example
- We regularly measure and monitor all that we do to gauge performance and excellence
- We make thoughtful but quick decisions and we take action
- We are flexible, agile and nimble but we exhibit structure and discipline in all that we do
- We are very passionate about student success
- We embrace teamwork and strongly encourage open communication
- We integrate regulatory compliance in all that we do and never settle for less
- We have an appetite for growth with quality and integrity
- We are always hungry for more
- We will never be perfect and know we can always improve
- We learn and grow from our mistakes
- We always embrace greatness
- We make grass-roots investments that lead to student and employee success
- We have a sense of urgency
- We take personal accountability and look within for solutions
- We attract, hire, and develop the best talent
- We seek support and assistance when needed
- We promote from within
- We empower "all" of our people to take ownership and serve
- We praise in public and coach in private
- We are close to our business and we know the numbers
- We have enterprise-wide transparency

- We face and accept the brutal facts and take action to address them effectively
- We follow up and follow through on our commitments, priorities and responsibilities
- Our team at the corporate office is aligned to serve and support the campuses
- We are mindful of the big picture, which keeps us focused at all times
- We exhibit determination in all that we do; we never give up
- We demonstrate strong communication and common goals between departments; no silos
- We focus on all levels of our educational model to provide a top quality student experience
- We have fun as a team and enjoy what we do
- We focus on fundamentals
- We are deliberate in our actions; always focused on results
- We are high energy
- We have a positive attitude
- We have caring, supportive, and nurturing environments
- We are super competitive
- We always focus on our core competencies with students being at the heart of our enterprise
- We take deliberate steps to celebrate achievements regularly
- We operate under " One Standard of Excellence" in all that we do within all departments
- We take pride in our work
- We are 24/7
- We are "grown-ups"
- We are respectful
- We are professional

We are IEC

175

Made in the USA
Middletown, DE
30 August 2019